What to sow, grow and do

First published in 2022 by Frances Lincoln
an imprint of The Quarto Group.
The Old Brewery, 6 Blundell Street,
London, N7 9BH, United Kingdom
www.Quarto.com

A Bloom book for Frances Lincoln
Bloom is an independent publisher for gardeners, plant admirers,
nature lovers and outdoor adventurers. Alongside books and stationery,
we publish a seasonal print magazine that brings together expert
gardening advice and creative explorations of the natural world.
Bloom celebrates all green spaces, from wilderness to windowsills,
and inspires everyone to bring more nature into their lives.
www.bloommag.co.uk | @bloom_the_magazine

Text © 2022 Benjamin Pope
Photography © 2022 Kim Lightbody

Commissioning editor Zena Alkayat
Designer Sarah Pyke
Photographer Kim Lightbody
Proofreader Zia Allaway
Indexer Michèle Clarke

A catalogue record for this book is available from the British Library.
ISBN 978-0-7112-69934

Printed in China

A seasonal garden guide

What to *sow, grow* and *do*

Benjamin Pope
Photography by Kim Lightbody

Contents

Foreword

I met Benjamin Pope in 2007 and was immediately impressed by his gardening knowledge, enthusiasm and attention to detail. Since then, I have followed his illustrious career with interest, a highlight of which is undoubtedly this unique and beautiful book, which will be invaluable to all gardeners.

Using the garden where he has worked for over 14 years as his canvas, Ben has continued to develop his eye for artistry and adventurousness in planting, gardening and even cooking with seasonal harvests. He has been responsible for bringing a rather neglected garden back to life by implementing new ideas and keeping up a high standard of maintenance, as well as extending seasonal interest and ensuring a consistent supply of vegetables and fruit to the kitchen, and cut flowers for the home.

Ben's gardening, teaching and writing experience come together in this very thorough book, which covers so much ground, from an indispensable sowing guide and advice on pruning through to techniques on making plant supports and the art of encouraging beneficial insects. For most keen gardeners, plants are an addiction and Ben seeks out seeks out worthwhile favourites, sharing information on how to grow and maintain them. Altogether, it culminates in a book that I'm sure will be a treasured addition to the library for both novice and experienced gardeners.

Rosemary Alexander
Founder of the English Gardening School

Introduction

Forget green fingers, for me gardening is about observation and really looking at the world around us – and by 'looking' I also mean listening, smelling, touching and sometimes tasting. Gardening is about noticing the beauty and seasonal changes in leaves, flowers, fruits and seeds, in the ground beneath our feet and in the wildlife that fills our environment. It's about learning to read the signs that can tell us if a plant needs water or if the soil is compacted, and then knowing how best to respond.

Gardening came into my life during my year out. I had postponed studying at university to instead work at a garden centre; it's there that I became seduced by the sheer variety of flowers and plants. Now, twenty or so years on, I am the head gardener of a private home in West Sussex and I'm still amazed and excited by (and in love with) gardens, plants and the wider landscapes they grow in. At the risk of sounding a little sentimental, I believe there's a gardening seed inside all of us: given the right set of circumstances, it germinates, reigniting a primeval connection with the natural world and a love for gardens and growing. The simple fact that you are holding this book in your hands and reading these words means that your seedling has already begun to grow.

One of the most amazing things about gardening is that you never stop learning – there is always a new plant to discover or a method of growing to perfect. Years pass and seasons change, but no two are ever the same. This variety of experience and unpredictability is part of what keeps gardening so exciting. There are so many magical moments in gardening, be it a beautifully frosted seedhead catching the morning light or the sweet fragrance of a rose on a balmy summer evening, or even the flavour of a warm, sun-ripened tomato that's been freshly picked. I find these moments satisfying and life affirming, they are experiences that you simply can't buy and are there for all to enjoy and share with others.

As you continue to garden – whether that's tending a houseplant on your desk or a fruit tree in your allotment – you also become part of a wonderful community of people who are more than happy to share their enthusiasm and interest in plants. I consider myself so fortunate to have found this gardening community early on and I can't imagine life without it. What I do remember from the early days of my gardening journey is the immense mountain of information that seemed so new: long Latin names, technical sowing dates, methods of pruning and advice on techniques and timings. It can all seem a little daunting, but that is what this book is for – it's a guide that will take you gently through the growing year and point you towards the things that you can do to encourage a flourishing garden.

The pages are divided into seasons (early and late) and each includes a Plants in Season section that celebrates the stars that shine at that time of year. This is followed by tasks that can be completed in the garden. There are also a few pages detailing what to look for in the wider natural world and how to celebrate and get the best from the season's gifts. Consider all of this a jumping-off point to help you find what works for you, your life and your garden. For ease of use there's a reference section at the front of the book detailing seed-sowing times and information on technical terms, along with advice on pruning and foraging. So whether you are looking for guidance or inspiration in a particular season, or hoping to move methodically through the gardening year, sit back with a cup of tea and enjoy the pages that follow.

A note on the seasons

In both the northern and southern hemispheres people will experience a change of seasons. These can be divided using three different methods: astronomical, meteorological and phenological. Astronomical divisions are based on equinoxes and solstices, however, there is disagreement as to whether these mark the middle or the beginning of each season. Meteorological divisions use typical average temperatures, with summer being the warmest and winter being the coolest, but as erratic climate patterns become more common, the weather we experience doesn't always fit the meteorological season. Phenological divisions use biological and ecological indicators, such as the falling of leaves in autumn or the migration of birds to warmer climates in winter. This method observes what is actually happening in the moment.

Successful gardening has a lot to do with timing and responding to how plants are behaving in relation to the weather. I believe it is the best and most natural way to garden. With this in mind, this book's chapters are divided into seasons rather than calendar months, so that the tasks will always be appropriate. The table below indicates the meteorological months assigned to each season and also what is likely to be happening in gardens in the northern hemisphere.

A note on hardiness ratings

For each of the plants listed in the Plants in Season sections I have included a hardiness rating. I have listed the RHS Hardiness Rating (Royal Horticultural Society), as well as the USDA Plant Hardiness Zone (United States Department of Agriculture). These two scales reflect the minimum growing temperatures a plant can tolerate. The guides are available online and are easy to find. They will help you decide whether a plant is suited to the climatic conditions you live in.

A note on foraging

The most important factor to consider when foraging is correct identification, so only harvest a plant you can correctly name. If you're new to foraging, take someone experienced with you, attend a course first or research using books. Be selective about where and what you harvest: young fresh growth is usually best, preferably grown in your own or a friend's garden. If you're out and about, always make sure you have the land owner's permission, and avoid plants close to roadsides, farmers' fields or where dogs regularly walk as these can be contaminated. Most of all, be respectful of the plant and wildlife, only taking a little from each area ... unless you're weeding your garden!

SEASON AND APPROXIMATE MONTHS (FOR THE UK)	PLANT INDICATORS
Spring March to May	Plants come into growth with fresh foliage and flowers, as day length and temperatures begin to rise.
Summer June to August	Plants continue to grow, flower and produce fruit and seed. Temperatures are at their highest and the days are at their longest.
Autumn September to November	Plants focus on flower and seed production. Deciduous plants die back and leaves fall in response to shortening days and dropping temperatures.
Winter December to February	Most plants become dormant with some exceptions. Temperatures reach their lowest and days are at their shortest.

General pruning advice

Throughout the book you will see references to pruning various plants, trees and shrubs. This brief overview should help you apply the disparate bits of advice to your garden.

Before pruning think about why you are doing it and what outcome you want to achieve, as there is more than one objective and method of pruning available. The three main reasons for pruning are:

PROMOTE HEALTH Remove any dead or diseased-looking wood to promote the health of the plant, along with any crossed and rubbing branches that may cause damage to the bark.

PROMOTE VIGOUR AND FLOWERS Pruning at the right time can help to encourage strong regrowth. Removing old wood or the tips of branches may reward you with more flowers.

ENSURE A BALANCED HABIT Through pruning you can ensure a plant has a balanced shape that is conducive to its health and pleasing to the eye.

There are two main methods of pruning and in both cases the aim is to control the framework of the plant:

FORMATIVE VS RESTRICTIVE PRUNING

Pruning lightly when plants are young is known as formative pruning and helps to determine their future shape. Pruning when plants reach maturity is usually restrictive and can involve harder or repeated pruning to maintain a certain size or shape.

PLANT FRAMEWORK The permanent framework is the main branches and stems on a woody plant. They permanently define the shape of the plant and form the structure from which new growth will grow. The semi-permanent framework is the main branches and stems that form the structure from which new growth will grow; however, they are gradually removed to make way for new main stems, rejuvenating the entire plant over time.

How to prune

Always use the right tools for the job, either secateurs, loppers or a pruning saw, depending on the thickness of the stem/branch. Whenever making a cut, cut back close to the supporting stem or a leaf bud to avoid leaving bits of stem to die back. The angle of the bud determines the direction of growth; look for a bud that points outwards, away from other branches to encourage an open habit and avoid crossing branches.

Pruning can be very specific to individual plants, depending on their growth, habit and responses to being pruned. Some plants need little or no pruning, while others should be cut back hard each year or thinned from the base. Most won't die from being pruned a little so it's always worth having a go and observing the results. However, do avoid pruning any deciduous plants in the prunus genus during autumn and winter, to avoid the risk of the fungal disease silver leaf. A general rule is to prune trees, shrubs and climbers after flowering, although as a starting point you can identify which of the three main groups they fall into:

Plants that flower in winter on previous season's growth

Prune these plants in early spring after flowering. Some, like *Garrya elliptica* (silk tassel bush), require a gentle trim, while vigorous plants like forsythia may need some older stems to be cut low at the base and removed. Plants grown for winter stems – such as *Cornus* (dogwood) and *Salix* (willow) – fall into this pruning group, with most requiring a hard prune to encourage vigorous stems the following winter.

Plants that flower in the first half of the year on previous season's growth

Prune after flowering up to midsummer. This gives the plant enough time to grow new stems from which it can flower the following year. Examples include *Philadelphus* (mock orange) and *Ribes* (currant).

Plants that flower in the second half of the year on current season's growth

Prune in winter or early spring, before the current season's growth begins. After pruning, the plant will put on new growth that will produce flowers later in the year. Examples include *Buddleja davidii* (butterfly bush) and *Perovskia* (Russian sage).

Gardening terms

Below is a list of some common technical terms that you will see in the text and hear other gardeners using. If you are new to gardening it may be worth having a quick read through or referring back to this section as and when you need to.

Plant life cycle
—

ANNUAL A plant that germinates, flowers, produces seed and then dies within 12 months.

BIENNIAL A plant that germinates from seed and forms leaves in the first year, often flowering and producing seed before dying in its second year.

DECIDUOUS A plant that loses its leaves for part of the year in response to seasonal change (usually cold or drought).

DORMANT A period of time when plant growth is suspended, usually in response to seasonal change.

EVERGREEN A plant that keeps its foliage (usually green) throughout the year.

HARDY A plant that can remain outside all year and doesn't need protection against cold temperatures.

HALF HARDY A plant that will survive outside if protected from the worst of the winter weather.

HERBACEOUS A plant that primarily has soft green tissue (non-woody). Some die back to ground level annually during their dormant period.

PERENNIAL A plant that lives for more than two years, often many more.

REPEAT FLOWER The ability to continue to flower, or flower again, after a main flowering period.

SELF-FERTILE / SELF-POLLINATING A plant that can pollinate itself successfully (with the transfer of pollen occurring on the same plant) to produce fruit and seeds.

TENDER A plant that is not tolerant of frost and needs to come under cover over winter. It can also be referred to as non-hardy.

Plant structure and form
—

BARE-ROOT A plant that is supplied without a container or soil but comes with its roots wrapped in fabric or plastic; it is a traditional method of supplying plants, usually when they are dormant.

BULB / CORM / TUBER / RHIZOME An underground organ that acts as a storage device for the plant's food and energy for a complete life cycle.

CALYX Collective name for the petal-like leaves (sepals) at the base of the flower, forming the outer protective layer when in bud. The plural is calyces.

CORDON A tree trained to grow in a specific form with a single stem (or trunk) with tight clusters of small side branches.

CURRENT SEASON'S GROWTH Any growth that has been formed during the current growing year (spring to autumn). Usually soft and green, though on some plants this may have started to stiffen (lignify).

ESPALIER A tree trained to grow in a specific form with horizontal tiered branches growing off a central trunk.

FAN A tree trained to grow in a fan shape with long, flat, spreading branches growing from a low and central trunk.

HALF STANDARD One of several forms described when buying a tree. It is a free-standing tree with a single clear trunk that is free of branches for approximately 1.2m and holds a well-branched canopy that is often seen topiarised into a rounded shape.

LATERALS A shoot or branch growing out from a main stem, branch or trunk.

NEW GROWTH The fresh growth seen on plants during the growing season, commonly found at the outer tips of the plant, but can also come from older growth.

NODE The point on a stem where the buds, leaves and branches grow from, often marked with a bump.

OLD GROWTH Plant growth that is more than two years old and is usually found close to the trunk or base of the plant.

PANICLE A loose, elongated cluster of flowers appearing on stalks along a length of stem.

PETIOLE The thin stalk that attaches leaf to stem.

PREVIOUS SEASON'S GROWTH Last year's growth that has started to become rigid and woody and forms an outer skin or layer of bark.

RACEME A spire of flowers that are held close to a single main stem; examples include foxgloves and delphiniums.

ROOTSTOCK Refers to the roots and lower part of a grafted plant (which is two plants united to grow as one). The rootstock can be used to affect the growth rate, size and health of the overall plant. A dwarfing rootstock ensures the plant remains a compact size.

SHRUB A woody perennial that is naturally multi-branched; it is usually smaller than a tree.

STANDARD One of several forms described when buying a tree. A trained form with a single clear trunk that's free of branches for approximately 1.8m and holds a well-branched canopy.

STEPOVER A tree trained to grow in a specific form with two main stems that branch horizontally and hold tight clusters of small side branches, often seen forming a low fruiting hedge.

UMBEL A flower structure where clusters of flowers are held on stems to form a flat, domed or spherical head.

PAGE 14 *Miscanthus sinensis* 'Malepartus' and 'Kleine Fontäne' (eulalia 'Malepartus' and 'Kleine Fontäne')

Planting and propagation
—

COLD FRAME A traditional structure that offers unheated protection against freezing temperatures. It resembles a low greenhouse with solid sides and a clear roof that can be left open or shut.

COLD STRATIFICATION Providing a period of cold to break the dormancy of certain seeds or bulbs and encourage growth. This can be done in a fridge or by leaving sown seeds or planted bulbs outside in winter.

CUTTING A section of a plant stem (or root) cut from a plant that is then used to vegetatively create an identical copy of the parent plant.

DIRECT SOW Sowing seed directly in the location where it is going to grow and complete its life cycle. This is particularly good for plants like zinnias that dislike root disturbance.

DIVISION A process of lifting a plant (digging it up) and splitting the rootball to create two or more plants. Commonly used to split herbaceous perennials and ornamental grasses to provide more plants or improve vigour in the parent plant.

GRAFT Describes two plants united as one, with one plant grafted on to the roots of another. Often used in fruit, rose and tree production. The plants must be closely related for this to work. See 'rootstock'.

HARDEN OFF Gradually acclimatising plants to new conditions and transitioning them from a sheltered, warm environment to one that is cooler or more exposed. This can happen over a number of days with plants being brought back undercover at night.

HARDWOOD CUTTING A cutting usually taken in winter when the stem is firm with a hard outer layer.

OVERWINTER Describes the process of a plant surviving the winter months. Gardeners will need to overwinter tender plants by bringing them

PAGE 19, CLOCKWISE FROM TOP LEFT
Oenothera stricta 'Sulphurea' (evening primrose); *Persicaria orientalis* (gentleman's cane); *Verbascum* 'Spica' with *Echinacea pallida* (pale purple coneflower); *Colchicum autumnale* (meadow saffron)

Gardening terms

indoors, or help plants outside to overwinter by applying an insulating layer of mulch.

PLUG TRAY / MODULE / ROOT TRAINER
A seed tray that is split into individual compartments, so each seedling will have its own space to grow.

POT ON Transferring a plant into a bigger pot or container to encourage future growth.

PRICK OUT Gently lifting out seedlings from a seed tray, holding the leaves and then planting them individually into pots or modules.

SEED TRAY A flat tray to fill with compost and sow seeds into. Often used with propagators.

SEEDBED A prepared piece of ground with a finely tilled surface soil ready to sow seeds into. This could be a place to direct sow seed or it may be a temporary seedbed where young plants can be lifted and replanted in their final position.

SEMI-RIPE CUTTING A cutting taken during late summer that is from material below the soft tip but has yet to become hard.

SOFT-TIP CUTTING A cutting taken during spring from the tip of a plant where growth is soft and vigorous.

SOW INSIDE / INDOORS To sow seed into modules, a seed tray or something similar and then leave them undercover to germinate. This could be in a greenhouse or indoors on a windowsill. See 'undercover'.

SHELTERED A position that is less exposed to the weather conditions; it could be a little drier, warmer and/or protected from intense sun or strong winds.

SUCCESSION SOW Sowing the same variety of seeds more than once, leaving time between each sowing so that the plants flower or crop in succession to give you a long season of flowers or a long harvest.

UNDERCOVER A sheltered position indoors, often in a greenhouse, or alternatively in a conservatory or inside on a windowsill. See 'sow inside'.

Soil and compost
—

ACIDIC SOIL A soil with an acidic pH of less than 6.5 for most of the year; it can be sand, silt or clay based.

COMPOST An organic material made from vegetative matter that has been broken down by bacteria and fungi during the composting process. Often made at home in a compost bin, it can be used as a mulch or soil improver. See 'potting compost'.

HEAVY SOIL Also known as clay soil, it is soil that has a high percentage of clay, making it heavy and sticky when wet, and hard and solid when dry.

LEAF MOULD A refined type of compost made solely of leaves that have slowly broken down and decomposed. Brown, light and usually free of weed seed and disease, it is great for mulching, adding to potting and propagation media mixes.

LIGHT SOIL Also known as sandy soil, it is soil with a high percentage of sand, making it easy to work when wet, quick to warm and dry, but also prone to leaching nutrients.

MULCH A layer of material applied to the surface of the soil to prevent weed growth and retain moisture. Organic mulches have the added benefit of improving the structure, health and fertility of soils.

POTTING COMPOST A refined, professionally made compost that is weed and disease free and is used for pots and containers as well as in propagation.

SOIL / LOAM Made predominantly of sand, silt and clay particles, along with organic matter or compost. The structure is more stable than potting compost.

SUBSOIL The lower section of the soil that sits above the parent rock or basal soil but below the topsoil. It has fewer organisms and organic matter, though is often rich in minor nutrients and minerals.

TOPSOIL The top layer of soil that holds most of the soil life, organic matter and major nutrients. The depth can vary: thin soils may be just 8cm deep, while soils rich in organic matter could measure over 40cm.

Sowing guide

Knowing what to sow when can be a little confusing, especially as some seeds can be sown in autumn or spring, while others can be sown in succession through the entire growing season. Below is a basic guide suggesting what to sow during different times of the year. I've also included when to plant various bulbs, as these can easily be forgotten.

Early spring
—

Sow sweet peas into modules inside. Harden off and plant out during late spring.

Start off long-season vegetables inside. Sow into trays or modules for planting out after the last frosts. Examples include celeriac, leeks and kale.

Sow aubergines, chillies, peppers and tomatoes inside, pricking out and potting on as they grow.

Sow half-hardy herbs like chervil and parsley inside, along with early salad and cut-and-come-again leaves such as chard, mustards, radicchio and spinach.

Sow early spring salad leaves inside to later harden off and plant out after the worst of the frosts. These include rocket, mibuna, mizuna and mustard 'Red Frills', all of which can be sown again in late summer.

Direct sow hardy root vegetables like beetroot and parsnips.

Direct sow radish and spring onion, sowing in succession every six to eight weeks.

Directly plant spring varieties of garlic, onion and shallot, along with chitted seed potatoes. Do this into beds after the worst of the frosts have passed.

Direct sow broad beans and peas after the worst of the frosts have passed. You can also sow in modules inside if the weather is too cold.

Late spring
—

Start off tender and half-hardy annuals inside. Examples include agastache, amaranthus, antirrhinum, coreopsis, cosmos, cleome, nicotiana, rudbeckia, scabiosa, tithonia and zinnia.

Sow tender and half-hardy annual climbers inside. Examples include *Asarina scandens*, *Cobaea scandens* (cup and saucer vine), *Ipomea lobata* (Spanish flag) and *Rhodochiton atrosanguineus* (purple bell vine).

Start off stored and new dahlia tubers in pots inside.

Sow tender herbs inside, growing on in pots before moving outside once the warm weather arrives. Examples include basil, coriander and French tarragon.

Start off courgettes, cucumbers, marrows, melons, pumpkins and squashes inside. They will quickly grow and can be potted on before planting out after the last frost.

Sow brassicas into trays or modules inside. Examples include broccoli (tender stem and purple sprouting), Brussels sprouts, cauliflower and winter cabbage. Sow lettuce, chicory and endives inside (to plant out later when bigger) or directly into the ground once the risk of frost has passed.

Directly plant bulbs that are 'in the green', including snowdrops and fritillaries.

Directly plant summer-flowering bulbs such as gladioli and lilies.

Continue to direct sow successions of broad beans and peas, adding sowings of French and runner beans after the last frost.

Direct sow hardy and half-hardy annuals outside. Examples include *Bupleurum rotundifolium* 'Garibaldi' (hare's ear 'Garibaldi'), *Calendula officinalis* (common marigold), *Centaurea cyanus* (cornflower), *Consolida ajacis* (giant larkspur), nigella and annual poppies.

Continue to direct sow hardy root vegetables such as beetroot and parsnip, as well as bulb fennel and carrots. Sow further successions of radish and spring onion.

Early summer
—

Start off spring cabbage, chard and kale indoors, planting outside when plants are big enough to establish before winter.

Sow biennials inside or directly outside (with protection against slug damage). Try *Angelica gigas* (purple angelica), *Dianthus barbatus* (sweet William), *Digitalis purpurea* (foxglove), *Hesperis matronalis* (sweet rocket), *Lunaria annua* (honesty) and *Verbascum blattaria* (moth mullein).

Direct sow tender annuals such as cosmos, tagetes, amaranthus, ageratum, cleome and zinnias.

Sow summer salad crops either in modules indoors or directly outside. This can include further successions of beetroot, radish, spring onion and lettuce.

Repeat sowings of fast-growing annuals, this time directly outside into prepared beds. Examples include dill and nigella.

Late summer
—

Sow oriental brassicas and mustards inside, planting outside as they get bigger for cropping before winter. Examples include pak choi, mibuna and mizuna.

Sow winter salad leaves and lettuce inside and plant out when big enough. Varieties include 'Winter Gem', 'Valdor' and 'Winter Density'; also try endive, lamb's lettuce and winter purslane.

Direct sow green manures on to empty vegetable beds to protect and cover the soil over winter.

Sow grass seed to establish lawns or repair patches of wear; this will establish before winter.

OPPOSITE *Dahlia* 'Fascination'

Direct sow wildflower seed into meadows or prepared ground. Try *Leucanthemum vulgare* (ox-eye daisy), *Knautia arvensis* (field scabious) and *Daucus carota* (wild carrot).

Early autumn
—

Sow hardy annuals, along with perennials, trees and shrubs that benefit from cold winter weather to encourage spring germination. Sow into trays or modules and keep somewhere cold but sheltered from the worst of the frost, such as a cold frame. Examples include *Althaea* (hollyhock), *Aquilegia* (granny's bonnet) and *Persicaria orientalis* (gentlemen's cane).

Continue to direct sow broad beans outside so that they germinate and establish roots and a little top growth before the frosts arrive.

Direct sow hardy annuals outside for flowers next spring. Examples include *Ammi majus* (false bishop's weed), *Centaurea cyanus* (cornflower), nigella, *Orlaya grandiflora* (white laceflower), *Papaver commutatum* (Caucasian scarlet poppy), *P. rhoeas* (common poppy) and *P. somniferum* (opium poppy).

Sow half-hardy annuals into modules where you can protect them from frosts (such as close to the house or in a cold frame). Try *Cerinthe major* (honeywort), *Calendula officinalis* (common marigold) and *Rudbeckia hirta* (black-eyed Susan).

Start off autumn varieties of garlic and onion, planting outside

to establish before the winter weather arrives.

Late autumn
—

Continue to sow salad inside, including mizuna, hardy mustard mixes and rocket, along with kale. This will give you a crop of smaller salad leaves through the winter.

Finish sowing hardy annuals, trees and shrubs that require cold stratification to germinate. Sow into trays and keep somewhere frost-free, such as a cold frame. Examples include *Ferula communis* (giant fennel), acer and sarcococca.

Plant spring-flowering bulbs in borders and pots.

Sow sweet peas into modules and grow on in a place that's sheltered from frosts. Plant out in early spring.

Early winter
—

Sow peas in pots indoors for early pea shoots.

Sow microgreens inside (including many brassicas, chicory, lettuces, endives and ornamentals like amaranth) for winter cropping.

Late winter
—

Sow onions from seed either inside in modules, or if soil conditions aren't too wet, outside, thinning later for final spacing.

Wait for the day length to increase before sowing chillies, salads and tomatoes indoors.

Spring

Early spring

As the sun rises a little higher in the sky with each passing day, the daylight hours grow longer, brighter and warmer. I love the precious but fleeting moments when the returning warmth can be felt on bare skin, though in the shadows, cold temperatures remain unaffected by the golden glow.

The garden has been quietly resting through the long nights of winter, and this gradual change is very welcome. It's a signal to both plants and wildlife that the new growing season has almost begun and it is time to come alive. Leaf and flower buds begin to swell and bulbs lift their heads above the soil, preparing to entice any available pollinators with their spring display. The willows and hazels are some of the first trees to flower, their prized catkins quietly suspended from their stems. These are soon joined by early cherries, plums and pears, which present their generous blossom that epitomises the beginning of spring.

It's a time when my optimism and excitement for the growing season ahead begins to stir and when the memories of flower-filled borders and abundant vegetable patches come flooding back. It's now I consider last year's triumphs and challenges and reflect on how to improve and what to change. It's also when I start to tidy and prepare the garden before growth really gets going.

However, early spring can be fickle and caution must be exercised: cold nights can return with little warning bringing sub-zero temperatures that will halt any enthusiastic growth. Luckily, for most plants, a frost can be tolerated and is simply part of their natural cycle.

Plants in season

While many winter-flowering shrubs and herbaceous perennials are still offering interest, early spring marks the rise of the bulbous perennial. Like forgotten treasure, these energised bulbs emerge from the soil to bring joy and life in all shapes and colours – I find them such a welcome tonic to any remaining winter blues. They're great for adding vibrancy alongside early floral displays from trees, shrubs and herbaceous perennials.

← *Anemone blanda*
WINTER WINDFLOWER

A charming, low-growing, woodland perennial adorned with daisy-like flowers in shades of blue, pink or white. The flowers open in the sun and sit above a carpet of delicate, dark green foliage that persists into early summer before dying back to tuberous roots. Great in large containers, beneath trees and shrubs or naturalising among woodland perennials. Happiest in light sun to part shade, in any soil that does not does not sit wet in winter. Plant 'in the green' in spring, or plant corms in late summer (soak in water overnight first). *Hardy throughout most of the UK (RHS H6, USDA 6b/7a). H x S: 10 x 10cm.*

Camellia japonica 'Lady Campbell' ↗
JAPANESE ROSE 'LADY CAMPBELL'

A stalwart for the shady garden, this evergreen shrub will sit quietly through the year with attractive glossy leaves until late winter and early spring, when it comes alive with informal double flowers in vivid red. Useful for town gardens, a *C. japonica* cultivar can provide privacy and interest, while its slow-growing nature means it can be kept in a large container. It will tolerate pruning soon after flowering to restrict its size. Prefers light sun to semi-shade in most soils with an acidic pH. Buy container-grown plants in winter or spring and plant when the ground is not frozen. *Hardy throughout most of the UK (RHS H5, USDA 7b/8a). H x S: 3.5 x 3m.*

Cardamine quinquefolia
FIVE-LEAVED CUCKOO FLOWER

An enchanting woodland perennial that will slowly spread to form a soft clump in spring and then die back in summer as if it was never there. Its palmately divided leaves appear in early spring looking super fresh and green, soon followed by delicate clusters of pale lilac flowers that gently hang above the foliage. Suited to woodland- or cottage-style gardens and conditions. Performs best in shade to dappled shade in any soil with added organic matter, although it will tolerate drier soils. Best purchased and planted 'in the green', while actively growing, from late winter into spring. *Fully hardy throughout the UK (RHS H7, USDA 6a-1). H x S: 30 x 90cm.*

Crocus tommasinianus 'Barr's Purple'
EARLY CROCUS 'BARR'S PURPLE'

As a group, crocuses are so welcome in spring (loved by bees as well as people) and widely available in a variety of colours. This species is one of the earliest to flower, generally with pale lilac flowers, although the variety 'Barr's Purple' packs more of a punch with its vibrant petals. Very easy to grow and accommodating of most conditions, these bulbous perennials can be planted in containers as well as borders, and even in the lawn to provide colour and interest before the growing season gets going. Grow in a sunny spot in free-draining soil or compost. Purchase corms from late summer and plant in autumn. *Hardy throughout most of the UK (RHS H6, USDA 6b/7a). H x S: 5 x 10cm.*

Edgeworthia chrysantha 'Red Dragon' ↑
PAPERBUSH 'RED DRAGON'

A choice deciduous shrub with geometrically arranged stems that form a small, rounded bush with oval leaves. In winter, when the cinnamon-coloured stems are bare, tight clusters of furry white buds offer a decorative effect. As winter ends the buds begin to unfurl, revealing small, tubular flowers that are fiery orange and sweetly fragrant. Prefers a sheltered and sunny or lightly shaded spot. Happy in most soils, although dislikes root disturbance so best planted somewhere permanent. Container plants are usually available when in flower from late winter to early spring. *Hardy throughout most of the UK (RHS H4, USDA 8b/9a). H x S: 1.5 x 1.5m.*

← *Fritillaria meleagris*
SNAKE'S HEAD FRITILLARY

A most elegant bulbous perennial known for its nodding, bell-shaped flowers which have a distinct chequerboard pattern in white and purple and are held on thin stems above linear glaucous leaves. While this species is perhaps the most well-known of the fritillaries, there are several others that are worth exploring. Grows best in sun or light shade in most soils and will naturalise if left undisturbed, as often seen in meadows and woodlands. Plant in flower in the spring or as bulbs in autumn. The bulbs dislike being out of soil, so plant as soon as they arrive. *Hardy throughout most of the UK (RHS H5, USDA 7b/8a). H x S: 30 x 10cm.*

← *Hyacinthus orientalis* 'Peter Stuyvesant'
HYACINTH 'PETER STUYVESANT'

Hyacinths are fantastic bulbs for scent and colour and can even be grown inside for Christmas (see page 202). In the garden they wake in early spring with stout green points that push through the soil and give way to strappy leaves and a central flower spike. As the spike grows taller, individual flowers open releasing a sweet fragrance. 'Peter Stuyvesant' has striking inky blue flowers with an even darker stem, although there are many others to choose from. Use in pots and borders and cut for the house. Plant in a sunny location in any soil or potting compost. Buy bulbs in late summer and plant during autumn. *Hardy throughout most of the UK (RHS H5, USDA 7b/8a). H x S: 25 x 20cm.*

Iris reticulata 'Pixie' →
IRIS 'PIXIE'

A small, early bulbous perennial with all the charm and intricate details of later-flowering irises. Tiny leaves surround short stems that hold the colourful flowers upright. 'Pixie' is a lovely royal blue with a contrasting yellow band on the lower petals (falls) and soft feathered edges to the upper petals (crests). Best grown in a sunny position at the edges of borders or paths; they also make good potted subjects closer to the house. Plant in a free-draining soil to avoid rotting in winter. Buy bulbs in late summer and plant in autumn for an early spring display. Cover the soil/compost with grit or gravel to indicate their location and protect the early flowers against rain damage. *Fully hardy throughout the UK (RHS H7, USDA 6a-1). H x S: 15 x 10cm.*

Narcissus 'Erlicheer' →
DAFFODIL 'ERLICHEER'

A deliciously scented, bulbous perennial that can be enjoyed from late winter through to early spring. It's also ideal for indoor cultivation (see page 202). Long, strappy leaves emerge first, soon followed by flower buds on long stems that are vigorous and super healthy in growth. The double flowers are ivory cream with more intense yellow flashes towards the centre; they can fill a room with their sweet fragrance. Grow in full sun in any free-draining soil. Buy bulbs in late summer and plant in autumn. *Hardy throughout most of the UK (RHS H5, USDA 7b/8a). H x S: 45 x 10cm.*

← *Ribes sanguineum* **White Icicle 'Ubric'**
FLOWERING CURRANT WHITE ICICLE

A classic, spring-flowering deciduous shrub with a relaxed habit and soft palmately lobed leaves. As leaf buds break open in early spring, pendulous racemes of white flowers appear, hanging gracefully from the almost naked branches. The refreshing combination of white and green is very fitting for spring, however there are also beautiful red and pink cultivars to explore. This shrub will grow in full sun to light shade in most reasonable soils. Container plants can be purchased throughout the year, though they are best planted in autumn and spring. *Hardy throughout most of the UK (RHS H6, USDA 6b/7a). H x S: 2.5 x 1.5m.*

Prunus incisa 'Kojo-no-mai'
CHERRY 'KOJO-NO-MAI'

A deciduous shrub or small tree that's grown for its spring blossom and autumn colour. Unusual zigzag stems burst into life in spring with soft white to pale pink flowers that hang in clusters along the bare stems before the leaves emerge. During autumn there is a second display, as the leaves take on red and orange tints before falling. A great plant for a large container or small garden. Prefers full sun and can be grown in most reasonable soils. Container-grown plants can be bought throughout the year and are best planted during autumn or spring. *Hardy throughout most of the UK (RHS H6, USDA 6b/7a). H x S: 2.5 x 2m.*

Scilla 'Pink Giant'
SQUILL 'PINK GIANT'

A reliable bulbous perennial with vigour that slowly bulks up to form a wonderful carpet of flowers and foliage. Strappy, emerald green leaves emerge in early spring and sit neatly below relaxed stems that hold the star-shaped flowers. Darker in bud, the flowers open to a lovely soft pink, fading to white. Plant bulbs in groups or drifts below trees and shrubs or use in seasonal containers. Best in full sun to part shade in any soil. Buy bulbs from late summer onwards and plant in autumn for a spring display. *Hardy throughout most of the UK (RHS H6, USDA 6b/7a). H x S: 20 x 10cm.*

Things to do

Plant summer-flowering bulbs

Summer-flowering bulbs (as well as corms, rhizomes and tubers) are eye-catching additions to any garden or container scheme, lending colourful, striking blooms that are often tropical in appearance. They include plants such as gladioli and lilies, which are winter hardy, but also many of the warmer-climate tender plants like begonias, freesias and zantedeschia.

While the vibrancy of gladioli 'Evergreen', 'Espresso' or 'Plum Tart' are particular favourites of mine, it is hard to ignore the sweet fragrance of lilies such as 'African Queen' and 'Star Gazer'; more refined are the Martagon lilies, which add grace and charm as they naturalise over time.

Identify the top and the bottom of the bulb where the leaves will sprout (shoot) and where the roots will grow from. This is not always obvious but the shoot is usually pointed. Rhizomes and tubers can sometimes be planted horizontally.

Check the planting depth. Corms are like bulbs and should be planted below the soil, usually about three times the depth of the bulb/corm. However, many rhizomes and tubers sit just below the soil surface and don't need to be planted deeply.

Bulbs and corms like gladioli and lilies work very well in containers and can be planted beneath summer bedding plants or perennials, where they will happily grow up through the summer display.

If planting in the garden, ensure that the soil is weed free and loose. If the soil is very wet and conditions are cold, it may be worth starting the plants off in pots and growing them on somewhere a little sheltered. Starting off growth in pots also allows you to plant out the young plants into the borders at a later date. This will make it easier to position your plants, filling any gaps between existing perennials and summer bedding.

Once your bulbs are planted, it is good to cover the soil with an organic mulch, compost or soil improver, which will feed the soil and plants while reducing the need to water and weed.

Construct plant supports

As the growing season gets going, some plants will need a little support to ensure they grow tall and strong rather than flopping, or worse, snapping in the wind or under their own weight. While being practical, these supports can also look attractive, adding sculptural elements to the garden. Metal cages and obelisks can be bought ready-made – they're quick to install and last a very long time, adding instant structure – however, this convenience and durability can come with a price tag.

To give you their best, the supports should be constructed (or bought) and placed in the right spots in the garden early in the year, before the plants grow too big. The simplest and most adaptable material to use for plant supports is beanpoles (which are rods/straight branches of hazel) or bamboo canes, but you can also use lengths of willow or birch.

FRAME Support can be given to plants in pots by creating frames using willow, lime or any other flexible stems. Poke six stems around the outer edge of the pot, bending the very tops of the stems and weaving them together. To provide extra support, use more stems to weave horizontal rings around the frame.

CAGE A cage can be made from weaving brash or pea sticks (branched twigs of hazel or birch) together. Cut your sticks so they are roughly two-thirds as tall as the final height of the plant you're supporting, allowing some extra length for weaving, then poke the base of each stick into the soil surrounding the plant. Begin weaving the tops and then the sides, enclosing the plant as you go.

DOME A dome can be made using a similar technique to that of the cage. The pea sticks will need to be longer so that they can meet at the top and woven be

together to create a dome. Side stems can be woven together and additional small twigs can be woven in to add strength to the dome.

OBELISK A simple obelisk can be made using three to six beanpoles, pushed into the ground about 20–30cm apart to make a triangle, square or circle. Pull together the tops to form a central point and tie with string or a length of willow. If more support is needed, wind string from one pole to another.

RING Push poles or canes into the ground, using a minimum of three or four to surround the plant. Wind string around the top to create an outer ring that will prevent the plant from falling down. It may be necessary to create a second supportive ring half way up to support the plant as it grows.

Prepare plants for the growing season

Early spring gives rise to the new growing season as plants reawaken and prepare for growth. Look closely and you will see the various buds and growing points begin to enlarge and open becoming more conspicuous as the new leaves and stems get ready to emerge. This signals the perfect time to tidy and prep plants for the growing year ahead.

Cut back and remove the old and dead foliage and flowers from all herbaceous perennials. Remove anything dry and lifeless back to a living growth point, which is usually found at ground level. This improves the appearance, helps to reduce pests and diseases and also makes room for this year's forthcoming growth.

Lift and divide herbaceous perennials which have become too large or need reinvigorating. Using a spade, dig up the entire plant and then split the rootball into smaller sections, replanting the youngest clumps that have the freshest growth.

Prune any shrubs that require spring pruning. These will include plants which are coppiced and grown for winter stem effect and those that flower on current season's growth, usually later in the year. Examples include *Cornus alba* 'Sibirica' and *Hydrangea paniculata*. Always cut back to a healthy growth point and prioritise the removal of dead, diseased and dying material.

Repot any container-grown plants that have outgrown their space. Increase the pot size and use a peat-free, soil-based compost which is suitable for permanent plantings. This will encourage healthy growth throughout the coming year.

Mulch and feed your borders and containers. For borders, apply a layer of organic compost or soil improver. For pots, remove the top layer of compost and then replenish with new. This promotes healthy soil and increases nutrient levels, while also improving the appearance of the display, preventing moisture loss and reducing weeds.

Weed the soil surface of borders and containers now while it is still easy to spot them. Use a hand fork, hand rake or hoe; remove old leaves and detritus, along with any annual and perennial weeds. Not only will it make the garden look smart, it will also help to reduce future weed problems.

Task list

Jobs to do during early spring

1

Plant spring varieties of onion and shallot sets directly outside if weather conditions are mild enough. Choose a sunny area with free-draining soil. Alternatively, start them off in modules somewhere sheltered. The sets should sit just below the soil surface. Also plant spring varieties of garlic for a summer harvest. Good options include onion 'Sturon', shallot 'Longor' and garlic 'Solent Wight'.

2

Make garlic spray using a bulb of garlic (crushed or blended), 900ml of water and 30ml of unscented liquid soap. Leave to steep for a minimum of 12 hours before straining through muslin and storing in a jar in the fridge. Fill a spray bottle with the mixture, lightly spray on to newly emerging foliage to deter slugs and snails. Reapply after heavy rain.

3

Propagate herbaceous perennials such as helenium and persicaria. Dig up and lift established plants and split them into smaller sections, ensuring each section has a good amount of roots and buds. The sections can be replanted around the garden or potted up for planting later in the season. Water in well after planting or potting.

4

Crop the last of the Brussels sprouts and Jerusalem artichokes, along with any salad that you have managed to get through the winter. Continue to crop kale and purple sprouting broccoli, and rhubarb will be ready to harvest soon.

5

Plan summer bedding and container combinations, making sure you have the seed to grow the plants or know where you are going to buy them from, especially if there is something specific that you are hoping to grow. Plug plants can be bought now and grown on inside for planting out later.

6

Prepare vegetable beds ahead of the growing season by removing any old crops and weeds, along with growing equipment such as nets or posts. If you planted a green manure in late autumn (see page 168), dig it in now. Otherwise mulch the surface with compost or soil improver.

7

Chit your seed potatoes to encourage them to sprout, ready for planting. To do this, place them in a tray or eggbox and leave somewhere light and warm for approximately 4 weeks. Small nodules (chits) should develop – just two or three per seed potato is enough. Once chitted, plant outside, chits facing up (see page 71).

8

Organise your seed sowing by making a list of what you need to sow and when you need to sow it (see page 18 for a rough guide). This planning will ensure that nothing is forgotten and that you can prepare all the seed trays, modules and compost you need so that you have the plants and crops you want later in the year.

9

Dahlia tubers can be potted up early (into pots filled with compost) and grown indoors. Water and keep warm to promote strong growth, which can be used to take cuttings or to give them a head start, giving you bigger plants that flower early and cope better with slug damage. Only plant outside after the risk of frost has passed.

10

Feed potted plants with a granular or liquid feed to encourage healthy growth. You can make your own liquid fertiliser with the fresh growth of comfrey or nettles. Place the leaves into a large bucket of water and weigh them down with a stone. Cover with a lid to reduce flies and smell. Leave for about three weeks, then strain the brown liquid into bottles and store. Dilute with 10 parts of water before applying to pots, borders and crops.

11

Service any mechanised equipment or tools such as mowers, hedge trimmers, shears and secateurs, so that they are working and in good order when you need them. Complete any garden landscaping tasks or maintenance such as cleaning benches, decking or patios before plants get growing and work in the garden increases.

12

Begin sowing your first seeds indoors or in a heated greenhouse (see page 59 for tips on sowing). Sowing outdoors can begin later in the season when temperatures have warmed up. Leeks and early salads can be sown into trays, while broad beans, peas and sweet peas can be sown into modules or small pots. Seeds including poppy and rudbeckia can also be sown in trays indoors.

Celebrate the season

Early spring heralds a fresh start and the potential for so much change. For many of us, the key seasonal marker is the vernal equinox when day and night are equal in length. This moment has a dramatic effect on the natural environment: birds begin to sing louder for the dawn chorus, frogs and toads call for a mate, and bumblebees and brimstones (the first butterflies of the year) waste no time in emerging to enjoy the warmer weather. It's a great time to get outside, look and listen.

Life can be seen bursting forth from every corner and crevice, from the blackthorn and cherry plum that frame the sky with ivory white blossom, to the hedgehogs that scurry about the leaf litter following months of hibernation. It is truly an uplifting time that makes the world seem a little brighter and bouncier.

Harvest and forage

Rhubarb is always on the menu in spring and the most sweet and tender crop is often available to harvest (or buy) early in the season, providing it has been forced. Forced rhubarb is simply achieved by covering the crown of the plant in late winter with something that excludes light and protects against frost, traditionally a terracotta forcer. As the rhubarb wakes in early spring, it grows in this dark protected space, which allows it to remain soft and tender. By late spring the forcer can be removed so that the plant can grow normally for the rest of the growing season. Field rhubarb (grown without this period of dark) comes into season a little later in spring. Crumbles, pies and jams are the traditional recipes for spring rhubarb, though I use mine to flavour gin – it keeps that sharp aromatic taste alive so it can be enjoyed all summer long.

Another classic treat at this time of year is wild garlic or ransoms (*Allium ursinum*). This bulbous perennial epitomises early spring with its lush leaves that carpet woodland floors. Their electric green glow is an absolute joy to witness on a sunny spring day, and a good excuse to get out for a walk and enjoy some foraging. A small picking of pungently scented leaves and flowers will give you a delicious homemade pesto that easily competes in flavour with its domesticated garlic cousin by having a fresh, almost 'green' taste. After flowering, the developing seedheads can be harvested to make wild garlic seed capers, a delicious alternative to traditional capers with a salty, garlicky and sour taste. Pick off individual seeds, dehydrate them in salt and then pickle in vinegar.

Build a nesting ball

Early spring is all about preparation for both gardeners and wildlife. A creative project for this time of year is to build nesting balls that will help our avian friends who are preparing for the breeding season. These orbs can be hung from trees or bird tables and are stuffed with material that can be taken and used by birds that are busy building their nests.

1 Weave together small, pliable sticks (such as birch or willow) to form rings approximately 15cm in diameter. You will need at least three to form a ball. Be sure to use freshly cut twigs that are easy to bend and weave or the rings will snap.

2 Place the rings inside one another at different angles to form the outline of a ball – this may require a little adjusting. Once you're happy with the shape, secure the top and bottom of the rings with string, leaving a length at the top end to use for hanging.

3 Fill with natural fibres and material suitable for nest building. This can include dry grass, moss, dry leaves, feathers and fur/hair (a quick groom of a four-legged friend usually proves fruitful).

4 Hang outside to decorate the garden and provide a source of nesting material for birds.

Celebrate the season

Create a spring arrangement

Celebrate the fresh colour and life that's emerging outside by bringing foliage and flowers into the house.

1   Begin the arrangement by selecting a medium or large vase which will suit the size of your flowers and display.

2   Cut a few stems from a tree or shrub that is just coming into leaf. Hazel or birch work very well as the small green leaves decoratively glow on the ends of the twigs. Cut or buy your flowers. Using blue, yellow, white and green shades seems to sum up the season and a good combination could be *Anemone coronaria* 'Mr Fokker' (pictured), *Muscari latifolium* (broad-leaved grape hyacinth), *Leucojum aestivum* (summer snowflake) and a daffodil like *Narcissus* 'W. P. Milner'.

3   Condition your floral material. For soft-stemmed flowers this means placing them in a bucket of clean water and leaving them somewhere cool and out of sunlight for a few hours before arranging. For woody stems create a 2cm cut at the bottom of the stem to split it. This will help with water uptake.

4   Your arrangement can be as simple or as complicated as you fancy, but I like to use the woody stems to create an open structure that supports the riot of spring flowers.

Late spring

The lengthening days of late spring seem to have a dramatic effect on plants. Pockets of green foliage spread and expand at an astonishing rate, almost changing the appearance of the garden each day. I find this such an exciting time to be outside and I love the fresh and exuberant energy the garden holds.

Needless to say, my favourite colour is green and late spring has every shade and tone there is, from the solemn dark leaves of bay trees and *Viburnum tinus* (laurustinus) to the lush emerald fronds of ferns like *Asplenium scolopendrium* (hart's tongue fern) and electric lime zap of *Euphorbia palustris* (marsh spurge).

We are also spoilt by the rainbow of tulips, fritillaries and other spring-flowering bulbs. The prolifically self-seeding *Myosotis sylvatica* (forget-me-not) is a common sight, creating an attractive, low froth of sky-blue flowers wherever it takes hold, and it is beautifully punctuated by taller biennials such as *Lunaria annua* (honesty) and *Hesperis matronalis* (sweet rocket).

Late spring can be a busy time for the gardener and a race to complete any final preparations before the growing season gathers pace. I find removing the first flush of weeds and then mulching can save a lot of time later in the season. But with seedlings germinating, grass growing and planting required, it can be a little difficult to prioritise the increasing list of tasks. However, it is not a time to lose one's head. The longer evenings make it possible to potter about in the garden, observe developments and plan maintenance; with a cup of tea or gin and tonic in hand, this is the perfect end to a working day and helps to put everything into perspective.

Plants in season

Bulbs continue to be star performers as we move through spring, including numerous alliums, late narcissi and tulips. The range to choose from and possible combinations available to the gardener is vast and I always find myself coveting something new each year. Shrubs such as osmanthus, lilac and viburnums lift the garden's more permanent structure with their scented flowers, while woodland perennials, including brunnera, disporum, polygonatum and pulmonaria, make the most of the light before tree canopies close in.

Aquilegia chrysantha 'Yellow Queen'
GRANNY'S BONNET 'YELLOW QUEEN'

A cheerful take on the classic cottage perennial, 'Yellow Queen' forms a soft mound of divided, glaucous green foliage held delicately on thin stems. Flowers appear from late spring to early summer on branching stems high above the foliage. The petals are a soft lemon-yellow and have narrow spurs that project from the back of the flower, creating an intriguing display. Works well in herbaceous borders or a woodland garden. Plant in light sun to part shade in any reasonable soil. Raise plants from seed sown in spring or purchase container-grown plants and plant out in spring or late summer. *Hardy throughout most of the UK (RHS H5, USDA 7b/8a). H x S: 80 x 40cm.*

Brunnera macrophylla
SIBERIAN BUGLOSS

A useful herbaceous perennial that has clusters of large, heart-shaped leaves which are verdant green throughout spring and summer. From mid- to late-spring, light sprays of tiny blue flowers appear with the first leaves – these are more restrained and definitely less promiscuous than the common forget-me-not. A trouble-free plant that works well in mixed borders, woodland gardens, beneath trees or in sunny patches. Best in rich but free-draining soil in light sun to part shade. Purchase container-grown plants in spring or late summer; plant, split and divide established clumps in autumn. *Hardy throughout most of the UK (RHS H6, USDA 6b/7a). H x S: 40 x 40cm.*

← Camassia cusickii
CUSICK'S CAMASS

A tough, bulbous perennial with long, strappy leaves that are deeply folded along the central vein, which enhances their grass-like quality throughout spring and into early summer. During late spring, upright flower spikes stretch skywards as the star-shaped flowers begin to open. Very useful within borders or in grass, alongside narcissi and primroses. Will happily

grow in most soils but enjoys moist, free-draining ground in a sunny or lightly shaded position. Deadhead after flowering if you want to prevent it from spreading. Purchase and plant bulbs in autumn or container-grown plants in spring. *Hardy throughout most of the UK, except the coldest pockets (RHS H4, USDA 8b/9a). H x S: 90 x 40cm.*

← *Erythronium tuolumnense* 'Pagoda'
DOG'S TOOTH VIOLET 'PAGODA'

A choice bulbous perennial appearing in spring with a pair of broad, elliptical leaves, mid-green in colour and gently undulating away from the central growing point. Soon to follow are the yellow, star-shaped flowers that are held above the foliage on thin stems. They gently nod as the petals become recurved over time, proudly showing off the protruding stamens. A pretty woodlander that works well in a herbaceous border or in a more natural setting in grass and beneath trees. Happiest in a lightly shaded position in free-draining soil enriched with organic matter. Plant bulbs as soon as they arrive in autumn, alternatively pot-grown plants can be purchased and planted in spring. *Hardy throughout most of the UK (RHS H5, USDA 7b/8a). H x S: 40 x 20cm.*

Euphorbia palustris ↗
MARSH SPURGE

A zingy herbaceous perennial that is a glowing addition to the garden. During early spring, new growth begins to emerge from a central cluster of buds, building in size and vigour as the season progresses. By late spring the stems have reached almost a meter tall and hold narrow, fresh-green leaves crowned with plumes of vibrant chartreuse flowers. By summer the colour fades and the foliage turns a buttery yellow in autumn before dying back in winter. Striking in a herbaceous border or within meadow planting. Grows best in full sun to light shade in moderate to heavy soils. Purchase container-grown plants throughout spring and summer; best planted in early spring or late summer. *Fully hardy throughout the UK (RHS H7, USDA 6a-1). H x S: 1 x 1m.*

Geum 'Mai Tai' ↑
AVENS 'MAI TAI'

A gentle, clump-forming perennial that creates low mounds of soft green, lobed leaves. From late spring to early summer, flower buds gently hang on burgundy stems, lifting as they open to display a semi-double ruff of soft peach petals tinged with pink. A well-behaved, edge-of-woodland plant that's suited to the front of a border or a container, it also makes a pretty addition to a cut flower patch. Grows best in a sunny to lightly shaded position in soil that does not sit wet through winter. Purchase and plant container-grown plants in early spring. *Fully hardy throughout the UK (RHS H7, USDA 6a-1). H x S: 30 x 40cm.*

Magnolia 'Genie' ↑
MAGNOLIA 'GENIE'

A compact deciduous tree that is perfect for small gardens and makes a great focal point. It has simple oval leaves from spring to autumn, while in late winter large furry buds begin to swell on the naked stems, finally bursting open in mid-spring to reveal bold flowers that begin as blackish-red and shift to purple as they age. Give it a little shelter on exposed sites. Prefers a sunny position in any soil that drains freely in winter. Buy container-grown trees from autumn to early spring and plant when the ground is not frozen. *Hardy throughout most of the UK, though late frosts can damage flowers (RHS H5, USDA 7b/8a). H x S: 4 x 1m.*

← *Malus transitoria*
CUT-LEAF CRAB APPLE

A small and highly ornamental deciduous tree with a graceful spreading habit. From spring to autumn, delicate, deeply-lobed leaves adorn the stems, turning golden yellow before they fall in autumn. Late spring brings masses of tiny, white, star-shaped flowers, that when pollinated, produce small yellow fruits for autumn. Perfect as a single specimen tree for a small or medium garden, or beautiful grown in a group for larger spaces. Prefers a sunny position or lightly shaded spot. Plant trees from autumn through to early spring; container-grown stock is available all year, although bare-root plants are best and available in winter. *Hardy throughout most of the UK (RHS H6, USDA 6b/7a). H x S: 4 x 3m.*

← *Paeonia daurica* subsp. *mlokosewitschii*
MLOKOSEWITCH'S PEONY

A slow-growing herbaceous perennial with presence once mature. It emerges from the soil with deep red buds during late winter, which remain closed until spring when the broadly rounded leaves appear. From late spring to early summer large, bowl-shaped flowers appear with graceful, pale lemon petals anchored by a central cluster of mustardy stamens. Ideal for the front of a border or raised bed. Best in full sun to light shade and tolerant of most soils that are free draining and given a regular mulch of organic matter. It takes several years to grow from seed so purchase and plant container-grown plants in spring. *Hardy throughout most of the UK (RHS H6, USDA 6b/7a). H x S: 50 x 50cm.*

Late spring

Polystichum setiferum 'Herrenhausen'
SOFT SHIELD FERN 'HERRENHAUSEN'

A dependable, slow-growing, almost-evergreen, clump-forming fern that gives texture and interest to a shady spot. In late spring the new fronds enchantingly unfurl from a bronze and furry central rosette, gradually displaying their final form. Their architectural quality relaxes as the year goes on to form a soft clump of luxuriant foliage. A good addition to a shady border or container underplanted with early spring bulbs. Best grown in part to full shade and in most soils. Container-grown plants can be bought and planted during spring and summer. *Fully hardy throughout the UK (RHS H7, USDA 6a-1). H x S: 80 x 80cm.*

Rhododendron 'Persil' →
AZALEA 'PERSIL'

A deciduous azalea with fresh green leaves in spring and summer that take on shades of gold in autumn. During late spring, as the foliage is just emerging, terminal clusters of white, trumpet-shaped flowers with a contrasting yellow throat appear. The flowers are also fragrant, making this plant a great addition to the spring garden. Use in shrub borders or woodland planting schemes or grow in large containers in full sun to light shade. Prefers a moisture-retentive but free-draining soil with an acidic pH. Purchase and plant container-grown plants in spring or autumn. *Hardy throughout most of the UK (RHS H6, USDA 6b/7a). H x S: 2 x 1.5m.*

Tulipa 'Black Hero'
TULIP 'BLACK HERO'

Tulips come in all manner of shapes and colours, and can flower from early to late spring depending on type. 'Black Hero' is a sophisticated, late-flowering double tulip with sumptuous, deep maroon petals and a light, sweet fragrance. Fantastic for adding drama to the garden. Plant in herbaceous borders, naturalistic plantings and containers. Despite being bulbous perennials, many tulips only last a couple of years as they dislike wet winters, hence the need to plant bulbs every year. Best in full sun in a free-draining soil where it may repeat in future years. Purchase bulbs in autumn and plant once the soil has become cold. *Fully hardy throughout the UK (RHS H7, USDA 6a-1). H x S: 50 x 10cm.*

Things to do

Sow seeds

Late spring heralds the longer days and warmer evenings that are conducive to growing plants from seed both inside in trays and directly outside. As a gardener, it's one of the most exciting things to do and I never get tired of seeing those first green shoots emerge. While it saves a little money compared to buying established plants, growing from seed also allows you to choose from many more varieties and produce larger quantities of plants.

At this time of year, focus on annuals (vegetables and ornamentals) and some hardy and tender perennials. Seeds that require extra warmth should be sown now and kept indoors or in a greenhouse. Fruiting examples include cucumbers, French beans, tomatoes and squashes, and ornamentals include cosmos, ipomoea and tithonia. You can begin to direct sow outside, too: in particular root vegetables such as beetroots, carrots, radishes and parsnips. Ornamentals to sow direct include bupleurum, nasturtium and nigella (see page 18 for a rough sowing guide).

Always check the specific sowing instructions for each type of seed, as both times and methods vary. Most seeds need warmth, moisture and light, but some, including many umbels, may require a period of cold to germinate. Other seeds, such as zinnias, dislike root disturbance and so should be sown into modules or directly outside, while actaea and hellebore seeds should be sown while they are still fresh (soon after ripening) to avoid drying out.

PAGE 57 Native *Anthriscus sylvestris* (cow parsley) provides a naturalistic companion to the eye-catching *Euphorbia palustris* (marsh spurge) **OPPOSITE** When sowing larger seeds and vigorous seedlings like peas and pumpkins, sow direct into small pots to give them more space to grow

When sowing seed, the common mistakes are sowing too early and too much. Seedlings can struggle during the early months of the year when light levels and temperatures are low, so it may be best to wait until conditions improve, ensuring that they grow faster and stronger. Keeping some seed back will mean that you can have another go at sowing should anything go wrong with the first batch, or you can repeat the sowing at a later date to help stagger the crop (known as succession sowing) and extend the harvest or flowering season.

Sowing seed in seed trays or small pots allows you to provide the right conditions for germination (they can be placed on a sill or shelf and moved as necessary). It also allows you to protect young seedlings from harsh weather and pest damage. Overfill the tray with a seed-sowing compost. It's quite important to firm the compost to prevent it sinking – do this by tapping the container on to the bench or table a few times or by pressing lightly with a tamper. Then level it by sliding a cane across the top.

Seed should be sown evenly on to the levelled compost. Lightly cover with compost, grit or vermiculite. Water from above using a fine rose or from below by placing the seed tray in a shallow trough of water. Allow to drain before placing the seed tray into a propagator, greenhouse or on a windowsill. Label the tray, recording the seed name and date sown. Check the seeds regularly, watering or misting to prevent drying out. Avoid locations that receive full sun all day and remove propagator lids every day or so to allow good air circulation.

Sowing seed directly outside may be necessary for plants that dislike root disturbance, this includes many root vegetables. Prepare a flat, friable soil surface and make a drill or small furrow to the required depth (as a general rule, larger seed can be sown deeper). Sow the seed thinly to achieve the recommended spacing required. Gently cover using the displaced soil from either side of the drill. Water using a watering can with a fine rose head to settle the soil (some people prefer watering the drill prior to sowing to avoid displacing the seed), then mark with sticks and a label, indicating what was sown and when.

As the seeds begin to germinate, they will require more space and nutrients for healthy growth. Seedlings growing in trays can be gently lifted out, holding a true leaf or seed leaf (small, usually round leaves that appear first, known as cotyledons) with fingertips and loosening the roots with a pointed stick or dibber. The seedlings can then be planted into a seed tray with cells/modules or small pots – use the stick or the dibber to make the hole. This process is known as 'pricking out'. These seedlings should remain indoors while they are small but can be gradually hardened off a week or so before you plant them out (see page 68).

Direct sown seedlings may require thinning out. To do this, remove weak and congested seedlings so that the remaining plants are at the correct final spacings, which will allow them to grow to their full potential. Be sure to water the seedlings after they have been pricked out or thinned out.

Encourage beneficial insects

With winter now behind us, the garden becomes a haven for many insects. As gardeners we quickly become familiar with the ones that are pests and feed on our beloved plants affecting foliage, flower and fruit. While an immediate reaction can be to squash or spray, a more long-term strategy is to garden in a way that encourages the natural predators of these pests, many of which are welcome wildlife or insects themselves. For example, aphids and slugs can commonly begin an assault on the new soft leaves and delicate growth points of plants at this time of year, and while a jet of water from a hose or an enticing beer trap can help, patience and time often allows nature to find a natural balance, with ladybirds emerging to feed on aphids, and hedgehogs and ground and rove beetles tackling slugs.

It's important to recognise the insects that are pests, but it is equally important to recognise their predators. Research the particular predator and understand their life cycle – this will help you to provide a welcoming habitat and spot them in the garden. Many insects have a juvenile stage, which may look very different to the adult stage (ladybirds are a great example of this). It is important to know all of the insect's life stages so that you don't accidentally destroy the good guys.

While most pests get going in earnest in early summer, you can be encouraging predators to overwinter in your garden so they are ready and waiting to control any problems. Predatory insects overwinter as eggs, larvae or adults.

Providing a safe space for this to happen will ensure a strong population for the following year. Cracks and crevices in buildings, along with bug hotels will help lacewings, ladybirds, solitary bees and spiders overwinter in your garden. A pile of sticks and debris – either in the form of a habitat pile or dead hedge – will provide a safe space for many beneficial centipedes, and ground and rove beetles (see page 126).

Grow companion plants to help protect crops and flowers and to attract beneficial insects. Companion planting means growing two (or several) plants together that support each other, in this case, by deterring or luring away pests. By growing the right plants, you will also encourage adult insects into the garden, which in turn will create the next generation of predators. Achillea, calendula and single dahlias attract beneficial hoverflies; cosmos, dill, hydrangeas and solidago attract

OPPOSITE A bee enjoys the flowers of *Anemone blanda* (winter windflower), which open on sunny spring days

ladybirds and solider beetles; and fennel and knapweed are great for lacewings.

Avoid the use of any chemical pesticides as these will often affect many species of insect and toxic residues can remain in plant material for some time. Although spraying will often kill the pest, it could easily kill the predator, too, destroying the delicate natural balance that you are trying to promote.

Allow an area of the garden to grow wild and incorporate wildflowers that support a host of butterflies, moths and beneficial insects (see page 143). Leaving a strip or patch of lawn unmown can act as a habitat for wildlife and double up as a design feature. Yarrow and dill help to attract parasitic wasps, while angelica and dandelions seduce lacewings. If possible, a patch of nettles will provide early growth for aphids to feed on, which in turn attract ladybirds and much more.

Include a water source in your garden, as this will provide a home for a wealth of wildlife, including toads, frogs, newts and dragonflies, all of which will predate garden pests. If a pond is not practical, a shallow bird bath, trough or bucket will provide a drinking spot for beneficial insects and garden birds (see page 74).

OPPOSITE TOP TO BOTTOM Ladybird larvae predate aphids on young apple tree foliage; hoverflies visit *Oenothera stricta* 'Sulphurea' (evening primrose); and a wildflower patch can be an attractive garden feature when shaped with mown paths and edges

Grow herbs

Nothing tastes better than fresh, homegrown produce, and as every chef knows, herbs are essential in elevating the flavour of a dish. While being expensive to buy, fresh herbs are easy to grow, attractive in the garden and many take up very little space. With a bit of thought, it's possible to create a scented display that will decorate an easy-access spot by a door or window and provide delicious flavours for months.

1   Decide on the type of container you wish to use. Hanging baskets and window boxes can be very convenient, or you may want to go bigger and use a vintage bucket or trough, or larger still and create a raised bed. Alternatively, use small pots or containers to grow different herbs individually, though it is worth remembering that small containers require watering more often. Larger herbs such as lemon verbena, lovage and Welsh onion can be grown in the garden alongside ornamental plants or in larger containers. Ensure your container has adequate drainage holes and place a couple of crocks or layer of gravel in the base before filling with a peat-free potting mix.

2   Consider which herbs and combinations you'd like to grow. Some herbs are thugs and should be grown separately. Mint is especially invasive and so should be given a container of its own, preventing it from swamping other plants. *Artemisia dracunculus* 'Inodora' (Russian tarragon) can also be a bit of a bully, while herbs such as chives, marjoram and thyme are very good at self-seeding, so keep an eye on these to ensure they don't take over.

3   For mixed containers, include long-lasting structure in the form of rosemary, sage and winter savoury, before adding herbs such as chives, marjoram and thyme that will return year on year. Finally, fill any gaps with annual herbs such as basil, coriander and parsley – these can be easily grown from seed and then planted out when large enough to fend for themselves. Allow space for growth and remember that some of the annual herbs may be tender, so you'll need to bring them under cover if a late frost is forecast. They may also need replacing during the growing season if changeable weather causes them to bolt and flower early.

4   While it's important to grow the herbs you are most likely to use, there are other benefits that you can take advantage of. Some varieties, such as *Salvia officinalis* 'Purpurascens' (purple sage) and *Origanum vulgare* 'Country Cream' (oregano 'Country

Cream'), have attractive foliage, most have medicinal qualities, and many have attractive flowers that are also appreciated by pollinating and beneficial insects, so leaving some to flower is a win-win.

5   Remember to harvest regularly to promote fresh new growth and prevent flowering, unless growing for seed, as in the case of coriander or dill whose seeds are delicious.

6   You may want to feed the plants during the growing season using an organic liquid fertiliser, which can be added to the watering can.

7   Herbs growing in containers will benefit from being repotted every year or so, just before plants come into growth in spring. Gently lift any plants and remove some of the old potting mix from the container before replacing it with fresh compost. The existing perennial herbs can be replanted and, as before, new annual plants can be added.

TOP Frothy white clouds of flowering coriander look attractive and encourage beneficial insects
OPPOSITE An old vegetable rack mounted on the side of the house provides the perfect space for growing a selection of herbs

Task list

Jobs to do during late spring

1

Begin hardening off plants that have been grown protected indoors. This means slowly acclimatising them to outside conditions. For seedlings, bring them out of the propagator during the day and back in at night. For greenhouse plants, open the doors and windows during the day and close at night. For young plants indoors, bring them out during the day and back indoors at night. After four or five days the plants can be left in their new position, though be aware of sudden frosts.

2

Prune mophead hydrangeas (*H. macrophylla* sp.). Remove the old flower stems by cutting below to the next pair of buds. Also remove up to one quarter of the plant, selecting the oldest growth and cutting it low at the base. This will rejuvenate the hydrangea and encourage better flowering in the years to come.

3

Redefine the edges of your lawn. This not only gives the garden a tidy feel, but also prevents grass escaping into the borders and becoming a problem among plants. Use a half moon or spade to vertically cut the side of the lawn. If you're cutting straight edges, lay a flat board down to help guide you. For curved edges use thick string or a length of hose laid on the grass (anchored with pegs or sticks if needed) to define the shape before cutting. Tidy by removing offcuts and trimming with edging shears.

4

Begin cropping early salad leaves and radishes, especially those that have been grown undercover with protection from the cold. Asparagus and rhubarb should also be harvested now (providing the plants are well established), along with the last of the kale and purple sprouting broccoli.

5

Weed borders and vegetable patches now to prevent annual weeds from flowering and perennial ones from becoming too established. On sunny days, annual weeds can be hoed off quickly, while perennials will require digging out with a hand or border fork.

6

Plant any new herbaceous perennial and annual plants in borders and pots, taking advantage of the good growing conditions. This will allow them to establish a little before the heat of summer arrives.

Things to do

7

Be mindful of late frosts and consider waiting a little longer to plant very tender plants or else have a plan ready in case a frost should be forecast. Canes with old bedsheets draped over can be a good solution. Alternatively, horticultural fleece can be used to create an emergency shelter if needed.

8

As the days become warmer it's important to ventilate growing structures such as greenhouses, cold frames and cloches. This will ensure the plants grow strong and reduces the risk of fungal diseases. If evening temperatures are still cold, remember to close the structures at night.

9

If you haven't already done so, pot up dahlia tubers (see page 43). As the plants come into growth be sure to keep them watered and acclimatise them to the outside in a sunny position. Protect from any freezing temperatures and plant them out in the garden once the risk of frost has passed.

10

Now the soil has warmed, plant potatoes that have been chitted (see page 43). A rough guide is to plant 35cm apart within a row and approximately 10–12cm deep. Multiple rows should be spaced 70–80cm apart. Allow space for earthing up later in the year, which involves raking the soil up to create a ridge that promotes rooting from the stem, producing more potatoes.

11

Take advantage of the season and enjoy the flowers of spring bulbs before they fade away, making a note of any that you would like to order and grow for next spring (such as the beautiful tulip 'Black Parrot', pictured). Many gardens have bulb festivals that you can visit for inspiration and to find out about interesting varieties and planting combinations.

12

Mulch borders with composted organic matter, such as rotten stable manure, leaf mould or spent mushroom compost. This layer of mulch (approximately 4–6cm deep) will feed and protect the soil, improving plant growth while reducing the need for weeding and watering throughout the growing season (see page 167 for tips on taking care of your soil).

Celebrate the season

Late spring is less about a fresh start and more about growth and potential. The ancient fertility festival of Beltane falls on the first day of May (or half way between the spring equinox and the summer solstice) and celebrates Bel, the Celtic god of fire, light and sun. It's no accident that this corresponds with a seasonal shift when day length and light intensity seem to dramatically increase. It's a time when flowers begin to bloom and wildflowers such as dandelions, foxgloves and sweet rocket fill verges and wild areas. In ponds, tadpoles swim alongside courting newts, lambs bounce around in fields and the first chicks can be heard calling from their nests. There are lakes full of ducklings and woodlands carpeted with bluebells – late spring is a fantastic time to embrace the outside world.

Harvest and forage

There is something special about eating new potatoes in season, especially what's known as the 'first earlies' which, as the name suggests, are the first to be harvested just ten weeks after planting. This group of potatoes includes the classics like 'Maris Bard' and 'Arran Pilot' – both have that typical firm, waxy texture and good flavour, and both are perfect tossed in a little butter and black pepper. More modern varieties include the multi-use 'Casablanca', which is ideal for chips and roasts, as well as boiled and buttered. 'Rocket' and 'Swift' are the quickest to mature and can be grown early from late winter – you can plant these in containers somewhere sheltered from the cold.

Another timeless spring flavour is that of elderflower. Late spring is when you can see the recognisable ivory white flowers that adorn these wild shrubs, decorating hedgerows, railway banks and woodland edges. Growing your own is easy and there are some interesting forms with cut or coloured foliage. *Sambucus nigra* f. *laciniata* (cut-leaved elder) has fine and pretty leaves, while *Sambucus nigra* Black Beauty (elder 'Gerda') has lovely pink flowers (pictured opposite).

Collect some of the flowers to make a cordial that bottles the delicate floral notes. For about 15–20 heads of elderflower you'll need roughly 500–800g sugar and 1l of water. Combine the water and sugar with the juice and zest of a couple of lemons or an orange, and heat until the sugar has dissolved. Add the elderflower heads, stir, remove from the heat and then set aside to infuse. The next day, strain and pour the cordial into sterilised bottles. Dilute with water for a refreshing drink or use to flavour cocktails, cakes and preserves.

Introduce a source of water

When looking to encourage wildlife into your garden, the one thing guaranteed to have the biggest impact is water. Whether it takes the form of a large pond or a shallow bird bath, water can attract and support so much life, from tiny insects through to amphibians, reptiles, mammals and birds.

BIRD BATH A bird bath is an easy and simple way to introduce water. They come in all shapes and sizes, though you may wish to get imaginative and use anything that can act as a shallow tray and hold water. Placing rocks in the centre allows insects to land and drink, and also ensures the bath is weighed down and can't be tipped over. Check the water level regularly during dry weather and replenish before it dries out.

WATER FEATURE These can be a slightly larger and more permanent way to include water. Again, water features can be purchased ready-made and may even include a pump for water circulation. Alternatively an old trough, tin bath, half barrel or ceramic bowl can be modified, providing it is frost-proof. Raised on to a bench or table they can look quite ornate, although this will limit access for wildlife. Position on the floor or part sink into the ground to improve access for animals such as hedgehogs, toads and newts.

POND, LAKE OR STREAM The most substantial water features are ponds, lakes and streams. Traditionally these were clay lined, but more modern materials are now available. Pre-formed fibreglass liners are durable and straightforward to install, but they don't offer the flexibility of a butyl liner, which allows you to decide on the size and shape. Formally shaped ponds and rills can be cast in concrete and then sealed, though even the most competent DIY-enthusiast may find this construction challenging, so it's best to employ a professional.

PLANTING To make any water source more attractive to wildlife it's good to include plants. Marginals or bog plants such as *Juncus effusus* f. *spiralis* (corkscrew rush), *Ranunculus acris* 'Flore Pleno' (double meadow buttercup) and *Trollius × cultorum* 'Orange Princess' (globeflower 'Orange Princess'), work well in smaller features, while larger ones can hold traditional aquatic plants such a waterlilies, rushes and water irises.

CLEANING It's important to keep the water clean and healthy and to prevent it from becoming stagnant. To reduce algae growth, avoid placing smaller containers in full sun for the entire day and incorporate plants and oxygenators such as *Ceratophyllum demersum* (hornwort). For larger features, a filtration system or natural algaecide can be used to cure and prevent problems with algae and blanketweed.

ABOVE A pond filled with lilies and water plants can permanently support an entire ecosystem
OPPOSITE A small enamel bowl provides a place for wildlife to keep cool, and is filled with *Rhynchospora alba* (white beak sedge) and *Lysimachia nummularia* 'Aurea' (golden creeping Jenny), as well as rocks and moss

Brew some weeds

Like all plants, the wildflowers that we often refer to as 'weeds' also enjoy spring, responding with lush, fresh growth and flowers. As well as supporting wildlife, some of these can be picked or dug up and used in teas, infusions and even brewing, creating refreshing drinks that turn your problem plants into useful herbs.

NETTLE Packed full of vitamins and antioxidants, *Urtica dioica* (common nettle) has been revered since ancient times for its many benefits, from improving bone density to providing a source of iron. Leaves can be picked, washed and then used fresh or dried before being added to soups and stews or made into a nutritious herbal tea. If that's not quite to your taste, add honey or other herbs such as mint, thyme or lemon balm to enhance the flavour as you reap the health benefits.

DANDELION AND BURDOCK Traditionally, the combination of *Taraxacum officinale* (dandelion) and *Arctium lappa* (burdock) were used to make an alcoholic mead, but today they're more commonly enjoyed as a tangy soda. Boil the roots of dandelion and burdock (about 100g each) in 1l of water. Add any other flavours or spices (star anise and ginger work well). After about 30 minutes, strain the liquid into a pan. Bring to a simmer with roughly 500g sugar and a little honey; stir until the sugar has dissolved. Pour into sterilised bottles and store in the fridge. When ready to enjoy, dilute with sparkling water; it also tastes good in whisky-based cocktails.

Celebrate the season

Summer

Early summer

After the surge of spring growth, the arrival of summer brings with it a sense of calm, as if mother nature has taken her foot off the accelerator. Temperatures intensify, creating drier conditions that cause many plants to grow a little slower and tougher. There is a steady pace as everything finds its rhythm.

At this point in the year, I always feel the emphasis shifts from growth to production as fruitlets start to develop and tubers begin to swell. This can also be seen in the environment around us, from chicks fledging nests to fox cubs learning to hunt – early summer is a time of plenty and full of opportunities.

In the garden, classic herbaceous perennials such as astrantias, irises and peonies adorn borders, working with the summer-flowering bulbs such as alliums, eremurus and ornithogalum. Shrubs and trees begin to make their mark, with cornus, lilac and physocarpus, followed by the sweetly scented philadelphus. Though above all, it is the rose that seems to relish this moment. Whether a climber, rambler or bush, nearly all roses have their first (or only) flush of flowers in early summer. There is a real sense of abundance and I love the old-fashioned, scented varieties whose fragrance fills the air.

As any gardener knows, with a garden full of flowers comes the job of deadheading. A worthwhile process of removing old flower heads that have begun to look untidy, while promoting the development of new flowers. It's an endless task, though enjoyable, rewarding and not that taxing. Despite the season's to-do list, there is time for moments of pause, to sit back and enjoy the garden as it comes into its own.

Plants in season

Early summer sees the return of many beautiful herbaceous perennials, lots of which have strong associations with the beloved cottage-garden style. While these plants play the leading roles of the moment, there is a supporting cast of annuals, biennials, bulbs and climbers all vying for attention. Flowers are in abundance and cerinthe, cornflowers and nigella joyfully fill gaps around campanulas, lupins and other border perennials.

← *Allium* 'Purple Rain'
ALLIUM 'PURPLE RAIN'

Alliums are brilliant additions to borders and plantings, their architectural flowers lending drama and colour. 'Purple Rain' is a bulbous perennial with open, spherical clusters of metallic purple, star-shaped flowers. The elongated, strap-like leaves appear earlier in the year and begin to whither as the flowers open, making this plant perfect among herbaceous perennials of a similar height. Alliums appreciate a sunny position with rich, free-draining soil. Plant bulbs in autumn or plant pot-grown plants in spring. *Hardy throughout most of the UK (RHS H5, USDA 7b/8a). H x S: 60 x 20cm.*

Convallaria majalis ↗
LILY OF THE VALLEY

A deciduous, rhizomatous perennial that confidently spreads to form large carpets of attractive ovate leaves, bottle green in colour. From late spring to early summer, simple arching stems hold numerous white, bell-shaped flowers that are richly and famously scented. Preferring a cool spot, it's best planted underneath trees and shrubs where it makes a tidy ground cover. Needs partial to full shade, ideally in heavier, clay-based soils, though annually adding a mulch of compost or leaf mould to lighter soils will keep it happy. Buy and plant bare-root 'pipits' in early spring or container-grown plants through the season. *Fully hardy throughout the UK (RHS H7, USDA 1-6a). H x S: 20 x 50cm.*

Digitalis purpurea →
FOXGLOVE

A classic biennial recognised for its stately spire of tubular flowers which elegantly droop from a central stem and come in shades of deep mauve through to white. After forming a rosette of textured leaves in its first year, flowers appear during late spring and early summer the following year, before the plant produces thousands of seeds and then dies. Perfect for the cottage garden, contemporary herbaceous border or wilder areas. Grow in part to full shade in any reasonable soil; can cope with a sunnier spot if given adequate moisture. Easy to grow from seed, although plants can be bought during summer for flowers the following year. *Fully hardy throughout the UK (RHS H7, USDA 6a-1). H x S: 20 x 50cm.*

Geranium phaeum 'Lily Lovell' →
DUSKY CRANESBILL 'LILY LOVELL'

An unfussy perennial geranium that sports both health and vigour. During spring, masses of fresh green leaves emerge to form an upright bush of foliage from which the flowers appear during late spring and early summer. Delicate and deep purple, the flowers are enlivened with a white eye. With a tolerance for part shade, this geranium is perfect for mixed borders or woodland planting. Grows well in most soils and will be kept happy with regular division and an organic mulch. Buy container-grown plants in spring and summer or bare-root plants in late winter. *Fully hardy throughout the UK (RHS H7, USDA 6a-1). H x S: 80 x 50cm.*

← *Iris germanica* 'Blue Shimmer'

BEARDED IRIS 'BLUE SHIMMER'

A timeless perennial with architectural, sword-like leaves growing directly from rhizomes that sit on the surface of the soil. During late spring and early summer, robust flower stems produce several generously scented flowers in succession. Unlike water and Siberian irises, bearded irises prefer a sunny, drier spot where the rhizomes can 'bake', so ideally place towards the front of a border or in a gravel garden in free-draining soil. Purchase container-grown plants in spring and summer, although specialist suppliers will sell bare-root plants in summer, ready for planting. *Hardy throughout most of the UK (RHS H6, USDA 6b/7a). H x S: 80 x 30cm.*

← *Meconopsis cambrica*

WELSH POPPY

A welcome, self-seeding and short-lived perennial wildflower that produces bright golden flowers with delicate crinkled petals sitting on slight stems above fern-like foliage. Flowering from late spring to early summer, these poppies prefer cool and damp conditions where their flowers will illuminate shadier parts of the garden. Perfect for a shady border or beneath trees, shrubs and hedges, they will also gently self-seed into cracks and crevices of paths and terraces. Best in moisture-retentive, free-draining soil in part to full shade, though will take sun given enough moisture. Scatter seeds direct in late summer. *Hardy throughout most of the UK (RHS H6, USDA 6b/7a). H x S: 40 x 30cm.*

Early summer

Oenothera stricta 'Sulphurea' ↑
EVENING PRIMROSE

Narrow green leaves with tinges of reddish bronze appear on similarly coloured stems in spring, rising to form buds from which large, fragrant, lemon-yellow flowers emerge. The plant flowers through summer, but individual flowers only last a day or so, maturing to a soft apricot as new flowers open to create an attractive display of colour. A short-lived perennial, it gently self-seeds if given free-draining soil and full sun. It is perfect for the front of a border or tussling with similar plants in a gravel garden. Sow seed in spring and plant out from late spring to late summer, allowing it to establish before winter.
Hardy throughout most of the UK (RHS H5, USDA 7b/8a). H x S: 50 x 40cm.

Rosa Gentle Hermione 'Ausrumba' ↑
ROSE GENTLE HERMIONE

Full of grace and charm, this small English shrub rose forms a relaxed bush of healthy dark green leaves that accompany the repeating flowers throughout the growing season. The petals are soft pink to pale blush and cupped together to form attractive double flowers that generously release a delicious myrrh fragrance. Best in full sun and happy on most fertile and free-draining soils, this rose will look good in mixed borders or a large container. Buy container-grown bushes throughout the year, or buy and plant bare-root plants in winter.
Hardy throughout most of the UK (RHS H6, USDA 6b/7a). H x S: 1.2 x 1.4m.

Rosa 'Paul's Himalayan Musk' ↑
ROSE 'PAUL'S HIMALAYAN MUSK'

A vigorous, healthy rambler with long stems that produce abundant sprays of small, pale pink rosette flowers during early summer that give an airy appearance and produce a sweet musk scent. Though it flowers just once a year, the spectacle and fragrance make this rose a popular choice for the romantic gardener. Best grown in full sun to light shade, it can be trained along a support or fence or also be left to scramble naturally up a tree (see page 89). Plant in most fertile and free-draining soils. Buy container-grown bushes throughout the year, or buy and plant bare-root plants in winter. *Hardy throughout most of the UK (RHS H6, USDA 6b/7a). H x S: 10 x 6m.*

Saxifraga × *urbium* ↑
LONDON PRIDE

A reliable perennial with attractive rosettes of evergreen leaves with scalloped edges. In early summer, dainty white flowers flushed with soft pink appear on lax stems creating a floral mist over the foliage. With a tidy, spreading habit, this perennial is perfect as ground cover, filling odd gaps and adding a little cottage charm. Use along the edges of terraces, paths and borders to create an informal look. Best in part to light shade in any soil that isn't waterlogged, though will grow in full sun given good moisture. Buy container-grown plants throughout the year or plant divisions in late summer to autumn. *Hardy throughout most of the UK. (RHS H5, USDA 7b/8a). H x S: 30cm x 1m.*

← *Syringa vulgaris* 'Madame Lemoine'
LILAC 'MADAME LEMOINE'

Inconspicuous for most of the year, lilacs really shine during late spring and early summer when they come into bloom with tightly clustered panicles of flowers. 'Madame Lemoine' has white, fragrant, double flowers that contrast beautifully with the heart-shaped leaves. Forming large deciduous shrubs, lilacs look good along a boundary or in a mixed border, providing they have a little shelter from strong winds. They prefer a sunny to lightly shaded position in any soil that is not waterlogged. Buy container-grown plants throughout the year, though the best time to plant is in spring or early autumn. *Hardy throughout most of the UK (RHS H6, USDA 6b/7a). H x S: 3.5 x 3.5m.*

← *Wisteria sinensis*
CHINESE WISTERIA

A classic, summer-flowering deciduous climber well known for its scented mauve flowers that hang elegantly from the stems before the foliage appears. There are many varieties to choose from ranging in size and flower colour, though all will require a support, training and pruning in both summer and winter (see pages 90 and 220). Perfect grown up a pergola or wall, although it can be bought as a trained, freestanding shrub. Plant in any free-draining soil in full sun to light shade. Grafted or rooted cuttings can be planted in spring or summer and will produce flowers much sooner than seed-raised plants. *Hardy throughout most of the UK (RHS H6, USDA 6b/7a). H x S: 10 x 6m.*

Plants in season

Things to do

Summer pruning and training

As the garden enters summer, many plants fill their allotted space with extended new growth, making the garden feel full and sometimes congested. A quick tidy and deadhead of spent flowers works wonders, though early summer can be the perfect time to selectively trim this excessive growth back and restore a little order to beds, borders and containers. With the use of sharp secateurs and a ball of twine, most plants can be sculpted or coerced into a form that is both pleasing and productive. When going about this work, I find that a gentle hand is best, as you can always cut away more, but you can't replace what you've cut.

SHRUBS Spring-flowering shrubs that flower on the previous year's stems (like forsythia and mahonia) require pruning now. Not only will it tidy their appearance, but it will also promote growth later in the year, which will go on to flower the following spring. As a general rule, cut back old flowering stems to a strong growth bud or stem, thinning out branches and shaping the canopy. For most, the complete removal of a couple of the oldest branches (cutting them off at the base) encourages new growth that will in time rejuvenate the plant.

CLIMBERS Climbers such as clematis, honeysuckle and wisteria grow vigorously during spring, resulting in wayward growth that can be easily damaged by a summer storm. For plants that are yet to flower, tie in the new growth to the supporting structure. For those that have flowered already, gently trim back excessive growth to a healthy bud. For more on pruning climbers, see page 220.

TRAINED FRUIT Early summer is the perfect time to prune established trained fruit bushes; these include cordons, fans, stepovers and espaliers trained over an arch, on posts or along a wall (note that freestanding apple and pear trees only need pruning in winter, see page 219). For trained apple and pear trees use the Lorette summer pruning method: cut all current season's growth back to three to five leaves to create fruiting spurs for the following year, while leaving all the older growth that will bear fruit this year. Many of the cut stems will grow more during summer, but the overall growth will be much shorter, which helps to restrict the size and shape of the tree. Apricot, cherry and nectarine trees are often grown as fans and will require a little more concentration: remove crowded branches to reduce the overall size but maintain the structure of the tree.

STONE FRUIT Cherries, plums and gages require minimal pruning once the main

framework has been established. As with all stone fruit, pruning should be completed in late spring or early summer to avoid the risk of fungal diseases such as silver leaf. Canopies should be thinned to increase light and air, so remove sections of congested growth back to a supporting branch, but avoid lightly trimming the overall tree as this will remove a lot of fruit buds.

CLIMBING VEGETABLES Long-season and climbing vegetables will often require some summer attention to ensure you get the best from them. Training and tying in stems of climbing beans, cucumbers, melons, squashes and tomatoes encourages them to climb well and reduces the chance of stems breaking later in the season. For crops like cucumbers and tomatoes, it may be necessary to remove small side shoots using secateurs. This will focus the plants' energy on existing flowers and fruit, improving the quality of your crop.

TOPIARY Trimming topiary is an important early summer job that encourages dense regrowth and a solid form. Using clean, sharp shears, clippers or a hedge trimmer, work around the topiary, trimming the current season's growth back to the desired size and shape. Using string or canes can help to act as a guide, though remember to step back regularly to check your work from a distance. Hedges and large topiary should be left until late summer to ensure you don't disturb nesting birds.

Water wisely

Water is one of the most precious resources on Earth and essential for plant growth. With its temperate climate the UK rarely sees a shortage in the supply of water and often this endless provision is taken for granted, although perhaps this is changing as our weather becomes more extreme and unpredictable. As gardeners and custodians of the planet, I believe we should all be aware of how much water we use.

The most effective way to water any plant is generously and relatively infrequently (rather than little and often). Ensure the water percolates deep into the soil or compost before leaving it to drain and dry slightly. This not only reduces water loss through evaporation, but also encourages plant roots to grow downwards in search of moisture. You may need to revisit each plant or pot a couple of times with the can or hose to allow time for the water to soak in and limit surface runoff.

If you're growing in containers, remember they are completely reliant on you to provide water. Size matters, as smaller containers will generally dry out faster and require watering more often. Grouping pots together will make watering them faster and easier and will also create pockets of shade that can reduce water loss through evaporation.

To help make the most of your water, use drip trays or bowls beneath pots, as well as mulch on the surface of soil. The trays will catch and save water as it drains away, while a layer of mulch keeps the soil or compost beneath cool and reduces surface evaporation.

Collecting your own rainwater is easy to do and beneficial for plants. Traditional water butts or tanks connected to downpipes work well and can be linked together to hold large amounts of water, though placing buckets and containers outside on rainy days is simple and efficient.

Surrounding impermeable surfaces with planted borders will reduce and slow surface runoff, giving your garden soil more time to catch and absorb rainfall.

Plants have evolved to live in all manner of locations and conditions. Spending a little time selecting plants that suit your growing conditions can save you hours of maintenance and, crucially, water. For a dry, sunny border, choose plants that have adapted to the conditions, allowing you to water them infrequently. In general, the characteristics of a drought-tolerant plant can include silver-grey leaves that reflect the light, long tap roots that can access water deep in the ground, and thick, waxy, succulent leaves that can store water.

Plant summer containers

I love to see the bold and elaborate schemes that adorn balconies and terraces at this time of year, enlivening blocks of flats and front gardens. They can be used to create a focal point and they also allow for experimentation; using specialised potting composts means that you can grow species that may not suit the soil in your garden. No matter the size of your outdoor space, there is always room for a pot or container.

1 Identify what your growing conditions are likely to be: the site aspect and position of the container will determine whether it will be a warm, sunny and dry environment, or perhaps shady, cool and damp. The potting mix will also affect the growing environment: a soil-based potting compost will be more free-draining than coir, wood pulp or wool alternatives. Also bear in mind that smaller containers will dry out faster than larger ones.

2 Select plants according to your growing conditions. You may wish to stick with a colour theme or instead focus on foliage and texture, but the important thing is to choose plants that will repeat flower and have a long season of interest. Among some summer annuals, add a few floriferous perennials, grasses or ferns to the mix, which can later be planted into the garden.

3 Place a crock or two over any drainage holes to prevent blockages then almost fill your container with your chosen compost. Arrange your plants while still in their individual pots, so that you can easily move them around. When happy with the arrangement, begin planting, securing the roots and filling any gaps with more compost. Firm the potting compost and make sure that the final level is almost to the top of the pot.

4 Water thoroughly. This will settle the potting compost around the plants' roots and within the container. As a general rule, water every three days in summer and feed with a liquid fertiliser once every week or two during the growing season to ensure healthy, vigorous growth and flowers.

5 In order to keep your containers flowering for as long as possible, remember to deadhead by removing old flowers and seedheads using secateurs or snips – cut back to a leaf or bud. Keep an eye on your container planting for pest damage, disease or stress and if the plants don't look very happy, try moving the container to a different location.

Things to do

An apricot and white display using *Calibrachoa* Can-can Apricot ('Balcanapt'), *Diascia* 'Aurora Apricot', *Nemesia* 'Wisley Vanilla' and *Sutera cordata* (bacopa), which provide soft colour and scent, and are enhanced by the silver foliage of *Helichrysum petiolare* 'Microphylla' and *Plectranthus argentatus* 'Silver Shield'

Things to do

Task list

Jobs to do during early summer

1

Now that the risk of a late frost has passed, plant out tender plants in the garden that you've either grown from seed or purchased as young plants. Cosmos, dahlias and tithonia are perfect for filling gaps in borders, while pelargoniums, plectranthus and salvias are great for pots and containers.

2

Keep an eye on weeds within borders and paths, removing them to make sure they don't compete with garden plants and set seed, creating future weeding work. However, leaving some weeds in lawns or in a quiet corner of the garden will help increase biodiversity and have a positive effect on your garden and its wildlife.

3

With the warmer and drier weather conditions, new planting will need extra water to help the roots to establish. (see page 93 for watering tips). Greenhouses and polytunnels should be ventilated and plants kept cool through regular watering. For greenhouses, apply shading paint, blinds or screens where required.

4

Now is the time to employ the 'Chelsea chop' – this means cutting back perennials that tend to flop later in the season such as asters, nepeta and phlox. Reduce all growth by trimming off the top quarter or third of the plant. The result is slightly shorter and sturdier stems and larger quantities of smaller flowers. This technique doesn't work for all perennials, so check online for specific advice. If you're still unsure, trial the chop by trimming just half the plant.

5

With rising temperatures, it is important to keep any eye on water features, ensuring they remain healthy habitats for plants and wildlife. Keep water levels topped up and watch closely for excessive growth of plants or algae. Pond weed can easily be removed (and composted), while a filter pump or natural additive can be purchased to control algae and blanket weed.

6

Monitor your plants for pests and diseases, many of which should naturally be in balance in a healthy garden with good soil and natural predators. For persistent problems the use of natural sprays, biological controls and physical barriers (netting and mesh) may be required. If aphids are beginning to trouble your roses use a hose to blast them off buds.

7

Tie in climbers and leggy plants that are growing rapidly on supports; this will ensure they climb better and stems don't snap as the year goes on. Examples include climbing beans, cucumbers, squashes, melons and tomatoes, along with ornamentals such as sweet peas and rhodochiton.

8

If you have a vegetable patch, it should be starting to produce an array of fruit and vegetables. Ready to harvest now are early and second early potatoes, along with beetroots, broad beans, carrots, courgettes, peas, spring onions, salads, spinach and radishes.

9

Early perennials that have flowered and are looking a little tired should be tidied up. Deadhead brunnera, geums and lupins for more flowers. Early-flowering geraniums can be cut back hard to promote a second flush of growth and possibly flowers.

10

Thin crops to improve the quality and size of the yield by removing some of the young fruit or vegetables. This allows more space and light for the remaining crop and will encourage the plant to put all its energy into the remaining fruit. Crops that benefit from thinning include beetroots and carrots, along with fruit such as apples, grapes, peaches and pears.

11

To keep plants in top health, add liquid feed when watering containers and potted plants, as well as hungry crops such as celeriac, cucumbers, squashes and tomatoes. Organic, liquid seaweed works well as a general fertiliser, although fruiting and flowering plants perform best with a high potassium feed. You can also have a go at making your own liquid fertiliser (see page 43).

12

Repeat sow seeds of fast-growing vegetables such as beetroot, radish, spring onion and salad leaves, along with spring greens and winter chard. Biennial seeds, such as foxgloves, honesty and verbascums can also be sown, as well as late-season annuals such as *Malope trifida* (large-flowered mallow wort) and *Salvia viridis* (painted sage).

Celebrate the season

Early summer sees some of the shortest nights of the year, which makes it a lovely time to be outside well into the evening. In the northern hemisphere, the summer solstice marks high summer, when the sun is at its furthest from the equator resulting in the longest day of the year. Since the Neolithic period, this has been a time of celebration and mysticism, and remains the perfect moment to light a bonfire and embrace the change of seasons.

On warm, dusky evenings, you may see bats hunting or hear the rustle of an elusive hedgehog. Out on a stroll, you can look for the light of glow worms or hear the call of a nightingale, especially in the grassland and woodland edges of the UK's southern counties.

Harvest and forage

Salad leaves come into their own around now and are much fresher and sweeter than shop-bought produce. They are easy and quick to grow, and there are many varieties to choose from. I always like to have a crisp, sweet cos or romaine lettuce available for picking, such as 'Little Gem' or 'Rouge D'hiver'. These taste good coupled with a softer, butterhead type like 'Marvel of Four Seasons', and enriched with spring-sown rocket, mustards and chicory. Try lettuces 'Amaze' or 'Freckles' for colour and interest, adding peppery nasturtium flowers and leaves, fresh coriander, aromatic basil or earthy beetroot seedlings. During hot weather, lettuce seed may be reluctant to germinate and many mustards, salad leaves and rocket will bolt. Repeat sowings throughout the summer will ensure you have a supply going into autumn, when winter lettuce, lamb's lettuce and mustards take charge.

Strawberries are synonymous with early summer, when they are most bountiful and sweetened by the warmth of the season. Great tasting varieties include the early 'Christine', mid-season 'Marshmello' and 'Renaissance', and the late-fruiting 'Florence' and 'Symphony'. Grow a couple of varieties to extend the cropping season, which runs from June to August. A personal favourite of mine is 'Mara des Bois' (pictured, bottom right), which has a gorgeous wild strawberry flavour and is perpetual, so will carry on cropping late into summer. As with any crop, there are some tricks to getting the best yield: avoid waterlogged soils and shaded sites when planting and use netting to protect from birds. A layer of straw around the plants will keep fruit off the damp soil, helping to keep it clean and dry, which can prevent problems with rotting.

Preserving flowers

It's easy to feel that the long days of summer will go on forever, but sadly the flowery abundance will fade. To capture something of the season, pick and preserve flowers so that they can be enjoyed for many more months to come.

Traditionally, dried flowers included helichrysum, statice and yarrow, along with ears of wheat and palm foliage. Thankfully, today there's a lot more on offer to inspire and it's worth experimenting with whatever you have growing. Mixing flowers like annual clary sage, limonium and roses, with attractive seedheads such as honesty and nigella will produce interesting effects. When selecting flowers, be mindful that their colours will often change, some quite dramatically. Strong, bright hues including yellow, orange, pink, blue and purple usually dry well, while white and very pale hues tend to look a bit dirty once dried. Very rich shades such as a deep red will often dry darker, appearing almost black.

The best time to pick or cut flowers for preserving is when they are fully dry, and this is usually during the middle of a warm sunny day. To air dry flowers, remove any excess foliage from the stems and lay the cut flowers out on a cloth or tea towel to allow any moisture to evaporate. Loosely bundle and tie the stem ends before hanging them upside down somewhere dry and airy away from sunlight. In about a fortnight, you should have dry flowers that you can arrange with. Add to other dried or fresh stems to create an arrangement, or transform into a wreath or hanging hoop.

To press individual flowers, petals or leaves, select thin, fully open flowers and avoid thick, succulent material that holds a lot of moisture. Some absorbent blotting paper and a stack of heavy books is all you need to press the flowers. During the early stages of drying, check and change the paper if the moisture from the flowers has made it damp – this will ensure the petals and leaves are preserved to the best quality possible. Once dry, they can be stored in an airtight container somewhere dark until ready to use.

Forest bathing

If you're longing for a deeper connection to nature, explore the Japanese practice of *shinrin-yoku*, which literally translates to forest bathing. Promoted in Japan during the 1980s, it was used as a form of ecotherapy to destress overworked employees, though its origins lie in the ancient history of many cultures throughout the world. In practice, it's a combination of mindfulness meditation and gentle exercise, in which you take time to simply be in a natural environment. Whether gently walking or sitting among the trees, forest bathing is an antidote to the stress and strain of busy modern life.

Most importantly, forest bathing should be relaxing, so find a wood, forest or green natural space that you feel comfortable being in. Visit different locations at varying times of day to get an idea of when these places are at their least busy, so you are less likely to be interrupted. In the UK, the Woodland Trust, Forestry England and National Trust have useful websites where you can locate forests near you; some even have recommended 'wellbeing trails', suggesting particularly peaceful routes.

Start off with a short session of perhaps ten minutes, gradually working up to a maximum of two hours. Turn off your mobile phone and other distractions so that you can focus all of your attention on where you are, and what you can see, hear, feel and smell.

At first it may feel unnatural, but the key is to slow down and focus on your breathing while keeping your eyes open to appreciate the leaves of trees and life that exists within the forest. Think about what you can hear and smell, how the sun and shade feel on your skin in the moment, and how you can tune into your surroundings more fully.

Late summer

As summer rolls on, the warm days and mild evenings encourage late-season flowers such as asters and dahlias to put in an appearance, while vegetables, fruits and nuts continue to ripen. It may feel steady and rhythmic, but in this latter half of summer change is afoot. The sun is still high in the sky but its rays are less intense, their soft tones often casting a magical glow on the landscape as dusk approaches.

Despite there being many sunny days ahead, the evenings are beginning to draw in as the autumn equinox approaches – a hint that it is time to take stock. Squirrels and jays are ahead of us, diligently stashing their bounty, while mice are busy foraging and feasting on whatever they can find.

In the garden, the summer tasks of deadheading, weeding and tidying continue, although now is the time to collect seed and take cuttings in preparation for next year's growing season. Organising sheds and storage areas is also important, so as the harvest comes in there is somewhere to keep the produce. Following all that spring and summer growth, the boundaries and edges of the garden have blurred and become a little unruly. To restore a bit of order, this is my moment to trim hedges, mow lawns and edges, and give the meadow its annual cut. I'm careful not to cut back too much, as at this time of year the garden should feel relaxed and unwound, like a leisurely Sunday morning.

It's a beautiful moment in the year, which gives me a chance to stop and take a breath at the end of the day, and time to admire both plants and the garden which, in this season's golden light, are shown to best effect.

Plants in season

Late summer sees another surge of flowers and the shortening days mean the rush is on for plants to flower and set seed. Most eager are the hardy and tender annuals, accompanied by many hardy herbaceous perennials and climbers. Grasses and naturalistic-looking perennials give the garden an easy-going appearance, though it still feels alive with energy.

Agapanthus 'Indigo Dreams'
AFRICAN LILY 'INDIGO DREAMS'

A restrained agapanthus with elegant proportions and thin, strappy leaves that appear in late spring to form a dense emerald tussock. During late summer, spherical clusters of dark, almost black buds open to dark indigo flowers held on thick, upright stems. Conspicuous seedpods follow; these dry and turn buff as the plant dies back in autumn. Perfect for a sunny, open border or gravel garden in a warm position. Prefers a free-draining soil; avoid waterlogged conditions in winter. Purchase pot-grown plants or plant fresh divisions in late spring. *Hardy throughout most of the UK (RHS H4, USDA 8b/9a). H x S: 70 x 40cm.*

Clematis 'Purpurea Plena Elegans' ↗
CLEMATIS 'PURPUREA PLENA ELEGANS'

A beautiful deciduous climber that flowers in late summer and is part of the viticella clematis group. It comes into growth in spring with delicate twining stems that gather pace and vigour as the year continues. From midsummer, numerous buds begin to form on current season's growth, opening during late summer to reveal small, double flowers of rich purple that persist into autumn. It will happily climb a fence, large shrub or tree provided there are wires or stems to cling to. Prefers a sunny to lightly shaded spot in a rich, moist but free-draining soil. Purchase pot-grown plants from late spring to late summer. Ensure the rootball is planted deep. *Hardy throughout most of the UK (RHS H6, USDA 6b/7a). H x S: 2.5 x 1m.*

Cosmos sulphureus →
YELLOW COSMOS

A half-hardy annual of modest stature that packs a punch from summer to autumn thanks to its glowing orange, sometimes yellow or red, flowers. Plants grow quickly from seed to form a loose cluster of fern-like foliage, continuing skywards with wiry stems that are soon adorned with the luminous flowers. Ideal for filling summer gaps in borders or containers, as well as cutting for the vase. Best in full sun in any reasonable soil. Buy plug plants or sow seed in spring, then plant out after the risk of frost has passed. Regularly deadhead to promote further flowering. *Half-hardy requiring protection from frosts in all but the mildest parts of the UK (RHS H3, USDA 9b/10a). H x S: 50 x 40cm.*

Erigeron annuus →
TALL FLEABANE

Like many of its relatives, this short-lived perennial daisy is prolific in its flowering, beginning in late spring and carrying on till early autumn. Germinating in early autumn or spring, it quickly develops a rosette of bright green foliage that soon elongates towards the sky, forming masses of thin, branching stems that hold hundreds of small white daisies with a sweet yellow eye. It's a great plant for filling gaps in borders and softening edges as it self-seeds readily. Prefers an open, sunny site on any reasonable or thin soil. Plants can be purchased in spring and summer or sow seed in autumn or spring. *Hardy throughout most of the UK (RHS H4, USDA 8b/9a). H x S: 1m x 60cm.*

Late summer

Gladiolus 'Espresso' ↑
SWORD LILY 'ESPRESSO'

Flat, pointed, sword-like leaves emerge in spring building in number and size until summer, when sturdy flower spikes rise up holding dark buds that open to rich burgundy flowers with an almost velvety appearance. A bulbous perennial that is a must for the cutting garden, it can also add seasonal highlights to a sunny herbaceous border. Deadhead stems after flowering and cut back foliage in autumn or winter. Grow in a sunny position in free-draining soil and mulch with organic matter annually to feed. Corms are available to purchase in early spring for planting later that season. *Hardy throughout most of the UK (RHS H4, USDA 8b/9a). H x S: 1.3m x 30cm.*

Helianthus annuus 'Ruby Eclipse' ↑
SUNFLOWER 'RUBY ECLIPSE'

A somewhat sophisticated sunflower that is quick to grow and flower from seed in just nine weeks, speedily maturing into a statuesque annual with a thick central stem and large, rough leaves. From midsummer onwards, multiple heads of creamy caramel flowers stained with dusky pink appear. Great for adding drama to a border, vegetable bed or cut-flower patch. Best planted in full sun in rich, free-draining soil. Purchase seed in early spring and sow, prick out and grow on undercover, planting out once the risk of frost has passed. *Half-hardy requiring protection from frosts in all but the mildest parts of the UK (RHS H3, USDA 9b/10a). H x S: 1.8m x 40cm.*

← *Hydrangea quercifolia*
OAK-LEAVED HYDRANGEA

An informal looking shrub with attractive stems covered in cinnamon peeling bark. In spring, large leathery leaves resembling those of an oak appear and create a textured backdrop over which clusters of tightly packed cream flowers gently bow. As temperatures begin to drop, the leaves take on fiery tones before falling in autumn. Good for adding interest and structure to a part-shaded area of the garden, either in a border or as a focal point. Tolerant of most soil conditions and prefers full sun to light shade. Container-grown plants are available all year and can be planted in autumn or spring. *Hardy throughout most of the UK (RHS H5, USDA 7b/8a). H x S: 1.5 x 1.5m.*

← *Hypericum* × *inodorum*
Magical Universe 'Kolmuni'
ST JOHN'S WORT 'KOLMUNI'

Unlike the classic St John's wort, this small, semi-evergreen shrub has a refined appearance, with both stems and leaves in a rich burgundy tone that bleeds into the burnt orange flowers. New stems emerge in spring, growing upright to hold clusters of the flowers during midsummer, followed by red berries that age to black. A long season of interest and healthy growth make this perfect for a mixed border, container or cut-flower patch. Plant in any soil in full sun to light shade. Container-grown plants are available all year and can be planted in autumn or spring. *Hardy throughout most of the UK (RHS H5, USDA 7b/8a). H x S: 60 x 50cm.*

Late summer

Itea ilicifolia →
HOLLY-LEAVED SWEET SPIRE

For most of the year this is an
inconspicuous evergreen shrub with
holly-shaped leaves held on relaxed
stems. In summer, terminal racemes
form on the current season's growth,
developing into cascades of lime-green
flower buds that open to scented, fluffy,
cream flowers in late summer. Grow in
a mixed border or shrub bed in full
sun to part shade. Alternatively, train
against a wall for a decorative summer
feature. Happy in most soils in a
sheltered position. Purchase container-
grown plants throughout the year and
plant in early spring or late summer.
*Hardy throughout most of the UK (RHS
H5, USDA 7b/8a). H x S: 3 x 2m.*

Malope trifida 'Vulcan' →
LARGE-FLOWERED MALLOW
WORT 'VULCAN'

An upright annual packed full of vigour,
with bright green, attractively lobed
leaves during late spring and early
summer, soon followed by large, papery
flower buds that open to reveal vibrant
magenta trumpets that are decoratively
marked with dark veins. A reliable
and generally trouble-free annual that
adds late summer colour in containers,
cut-flower patches and borders. Best
planted in full sun in any reasonable
soil. Purchase and sow seed in mid-
spring for flowering approximately
12 weeks later. *Hardy throughout most
of the UK (RHS H4, USDA 8b/9a).
H x S: 50 x 40cm.*

Persicaria amplexicaulis 'Fat Domino' →
RED BISTORT 'FAT DOMINO'

A burly herbaceous perennial with large, pointed leaves that gently hang to form a bed of textured foliage over which numerous thin flowering stems appear during late summer. The flowers are deep scarlet and packed tightly together creating an eye-catching display of vibrant pompom-like racemes. A reliable perennial that looks brilliant in borders. Prefers sun to part shade and rich to heavy soil. Lift and divide or purchase container-grown plants in early spring and plant out before the arrival of summer. *Fully hardy throughout the UK (RHS H7, USDA 6a-1). H x S: 1.2m x 80cm.*

Thalictrum delavayi →
CHINESE MEADOW RUE

Full of grace and charm, this dainty looking perennial is much tougher than it appears. Long, slender stems push skywards during spring and summer holding glaucous leaves that are divided into the most delicate collection of leaflets. From midsummer, airy clouds of lilac flowers appear with pronounced creamy white stamens that lend a mellow contrast. Perfect for adding refined interest to herbaceous perennial borders and naturalistic grass plantings. It prefers sun to light shade in moisture-retentive, free-draining soil. Purchase container-grown plants through the year and plant in spring or early autumn.
Fully hardy throughout the UK (RHS H7, USDA 6a-1). H x S: 1.5m x 50cm.

Things to do

Save and store seed

As the summer winds down, the race is on for plants to produce and set seed before the arrival of winter. Many plants will continue to flower if deadheaded, though doing this may prevent them producing the best quality ripe seed. Now is the time to think about what you wish to grow next year and any seed that you want to collect. As a member of the 'put another jumper on if you're cold' generation, I have an inherently frugal nature, and collecting, cleaning, storing and sowing my own seeds is a process I find immensely satisfying and would recommend to anyone!

Something to remember is that seed production is a result of sexual reproduction by plants, resulting in variability – this means you may end up nurturing seedlings that look slightly different from the parent plant. The degree of difference will depend on plant type and previous breeding, though from a relaxed gardener's point of view, this can be an exciting experiment.

Identify which seed is worth collecting. Annuals, biennials and some perennials may flower in the first year and so will be more satisfying to grow, giving quick results. In contrast, trees and shrubs can be slower and trickier to germinate and so will take more patience and experience. If you're new to seed-saving, start off with something easy and rewarding like cosmos, nigella, sunflowers or poppies.

It pays to be organised, especially if you are collecting lots of different seeds. Once you have decided what to collect,

ABOVE Angelica seedheads **OPPOSITE** Poppy seedheads which, along with alliums and thistles, make interesting subjects as they dry, so can be used as decoration as well as for seed production

create a list or tick sheet to make sure no plants are forgotten. At every stage, label the seed with the plant name. I also like to include the date it was collected and the location, so that you know its age and provenance.

When collecting, look for the best seed that is almost ripe and falling from the plant – this is usually from stems and pods that appear dry and dead. Choose a dry day to collect seed as wet conditions can encourage mould. Cut stems and pods, placing them in a paper bag or straight on to a tray lined with newspaper. Leave them to fully dry indoors for one to two weeks.

Once the seeds are dry, clean them by removing them from their pod or umbrella and getting rid of any other unwanted debris. Depending on the seed it may be necessary to sieve or winnow to separate any chaff and debris from the seed.

Cleaned seed can be stored in a paper envelope that's labelled with the relevant information. I like to store all my envelopes in an old tin somewhere cool, dry and away from sun to protect them from pests and damp. Some seed, such as hellebores, are best sown while still fresh, so check the individual planting advice before storing.

Take cuttings

As a gardener, the idea of creating new plants from existing ones through propagation is an exciting prospect, not only because it means extra plants for the garden, but also because it is an enjoyable thing to do. Whether you are looking to increase the size of your borders, fill your containers until they overflow or just experiment for fun, it's worth having a go.

For most plants, propagation usually involves seed saving (see page 114), division (see page 39) and/or cuttings. There are several reasons for taking cuttings, but essentially the aim is to increase the number of plants that you have, be it for insurance against loss (such as losing a tender plant to a cold winter), rejuvenation of a specific species (which may be rare or falling out of favour), to gift to friends, or to add more plants to the borders. The benefit of a cuttings (over seed saving and sowing, for example) is that the propagated plant is a direct copy of the parent plant, keeping the same characteristics such as flower colour or leaf shape. Once rooted they are vigorous in growth and will often reach flowering maturity faster than seed-raised plants.

There are various types of cuttings that you can take throughout the year. For many different trees and shrubs, soft-tip cuttings can be taken in spring and hardwood cuttings can be taken in winter. Root cuttings can be taken in late autumn and winter, and are a good method for some herbaceous perennials that are tricky to propagate by stem cuttings. Late summer is the time to take semi-ripe stem cuttings from the current season's growth of many plant species. Examples include both hardy and tender perennials (such as salvias, penstemons and pelargoniums), trees and shrubs (including hydrangeas and *Magnolia grandiflora*), climbers such *Trachelospermum jasminoides* (star jasmine), and herbs like lavender, rosemary and sage.

1 Take your semi-ripe stem cuttings in the morning, when plant stems are full of water. Stems should be firm but not hard, and these are usually found a little below the tip of each stem. Cut a length of stem approximately 15cm long. To reduce water loss, place the cut stems into a polythene bag and keep away from direct sun.

2 Next, prepare the stems for propagation. Make a basal cut directly below a leaf and also trim off the top soft tip, cutting just above a leaf. This should give you a stem approximately 10–12cm long. Remove one third to half of the lower leaves by cutting them off neatly against the stem.

3 Prepare a tray or pot with a compost specifically for cuttings. This is available to buy ready-made or you can mix your own: use 50 per cent peat-free compost with 50 per cent sharp sand or perlite (this aids drainage and increases valuable air pockets in the compost). Dip the base of the cuttings in a hormone rooting powder or gel before inserting the lower stem into the tray.

4 Water well and place either in a propagator, or cover the tray with a clear bag to increase humidity around the cuttings. Place them inside somewhere light but away from direct sun. If temperatures are low, use bottom heat to speed up the rooting process (a heated mat or propagator is ideal and a good investment for seed sowing as well as cuttings).

5 Watch for new top growth, as well as roots emerging from the bottom of the tray – this signals the cuttings have rooted. Trees and shrubs are best left till the following spring before separating and potting up, whereas perennials can be potted on in early autumn, provided there is enough warmth and light to help them establish and grow. They can then be planted outside the following spring.

Make your own compost

As the growing season begins to slow down, my thoughts naturally turn to the year ahead and what I can do to improve the garden. As always, promoting plant health begins with the soil; improving both its structure and fertility is a worthwhile practice and often the best way to achieve this is to apply and incorporate well-rotted organic matter. Soil improvers and compost can be bought ready-made, however making your own means you can utilise your garden waste and save a little money.

Homemade compost can be made throughout the year using a mix of garden waste (both green and brown), along with organic household waste. Whether you're hot or cold composting it's important to layer the waste and mix soft green material (that is often high in nitrogen) with tougher brown material (that holds carbon). Aim for a 50:50 mix, adding more brown material if the compost is too wet or more green if it's too dry.

COLD The cold compost method is the simplest. Once you have a suitable place for a compost heap or have invested in a basic compost bin, you can layer the materials over a long period of time. Naturally occurring bacteria and fungi, along with worms and invertebrates, will slowly decompose the waste. The initial decomposition generates some heat but it quickly dissipates leaving the pile cold, slowing the decomposition process – it can take anything from six months to a year to generate compost that's ready to use.

HOT If you are looking for a faster process, hot composting is a good option, though you will have to put in some effort as you need to mix the compost. You add material in the same way as cold composting, but this time you turn the compost regularly, mixing the outside material inwards using a digging fork.

Turning the compost helps to aerate it, incorporating oxygen that kick-starts the microbial activity into decomposing the waste faster. The compost is ready in as little as four or six months. It may be necessary to water your heap or protect it from the rain to maintain an optimum moisture content.

HOT BOX Faster still is hot box composting. In principle, it is the same method as hot composting, but involves shredding the waste first and then using an insulated bin to maximise the heat; some methods also use microbial additives to increase and speed up the decomposition process. Ready to use compost can be created in as little as six weeks. You can buy a specialist bin that does most of the work for you, although the process is far more technical and involved than simple hot and cold composting.

BOKASHI Originating in Japan, bokashi is a neat method of composting organic kitchen waste (though not garden waste). The bin can be kept in the kitchen and you need to buy ready-made 'active' bran to add to the food waste to promote the fermenting process. Once the bin is full and sealed, an acidic matter will form in about two weeks and can then be incorporated into flower beds and borders as a concentrated feed or added to your compost pile to enhance it. The process also creates a liquid that can be diluted and used to activate your compost heap or as a liquid feed for your plants.

Late summer

TOP A mix of soft green material for the compost pile **BOTTOM** A cold compost pile with green material, vegetable waste, chipped twigs, lawn clippings and cardboard (for cold composting, always exclude weeds and their seeds)

Task list

Jobs to do during late summer

1

Late summer and early autumn is the time to cut and trim hedges. The birds have finished nesting and the regrowth after cutting will be minimal, so the tidy appearance will be maintained all winter. Trimming now will also allow time for the cuts to heal before the frost arrives, avoiding any subsequent damage.

2

Vegetable beds and fruit bushes are full of produce and cropping at this time of year. Harvest everything from beetroots, carrots and salad through to Florence fennel, beans and aubergines. Currants and early raspberries should be ripe, with blueberries, blackberries, plums and gages to follow.

3

Now is the time to think about which spring-flowering bulbs you'd like in your garden, from alliums and camassias to narcissi and tulips. Look back at any notes or photographs you may have taken in spring for inspiration, and shop around and order now to ensure delivery in early autumn, ready for planting soon after.

4

Plan which fruit trees or bushes you'd like to plant in autumn. Bare-root plants can be pre-ordered now and then dispatched while they are dormant during the winter period. Many fruit farms will have tasting days or festivals at this time of year, which is a great way to try out the different varieties and flavours, and to find something that you love.

5

As summer comes to an end, plants can look a little untidy. By removing old leaves and spent flowers, you can make the garden feel fresh and potentially encourage the production of more flowers. Lavender can be trimmed back to the base of the current year's growth as the flowers begin to fade. This ensures a dense habit and good foliage for winter, though be mindful not to prune back too hard into old wood, as it will struggle to sprout new growth.

6

Meadow areas and patches of long grass should be cut now, as wildflowers and grasses set their seed. Leave the cuttings in situ for several days to dry, before raking and removing the debris to prevent enrichment of the soil. Any loose seeds should fall to the ground and be ready to germinate for next year's display.

Things to do

7

As with every season, it's important to walk around the garden and make notes on what has worked and what needs improving. Pay particular attention to borders, listing any perennials that may need moving, splitting or staking, along with seasonal gaps that you could fill with annuals next year. You might be confident that you'll remember, but if you're anything like me, the notes will prove invaluable.

8

Late summer is the perfect time to think about sowing late salad crops and hardy annuals, ensuring they get to a decent size before the winter cold arrives. Either direct sow outside or into trays and modules undercover. Mustards, rocket and winter lettuce will crop with very little protection, while some annuals such as agrostemma, calendula and cerinthe will form small plants that will flower early the following year.

9

Look over any tender plants such as nemesia, pelargoniums and plectranthus to decide whether you will bring them indoors for winter or propagate them and overwinter them as rooted cuttings (see page 116). Propagating them means you will have younger plants that will be full of vigour and get away faster in the spring. If you plan to bring the plants undercover, ensure you have containers to pot them into and space to house them.

10

With so much growing in the garden, it's easy to overlook the weeds, particularly those low to the ground. But just like your ornamental plants, weeds will be keen to produce and set seed for future generations, so spending a little time removing them now could potentially save you a lot of work in the future.

11

Now is a moment to clean and tidy greenhouses, cold frames or polytunnels before the weather turns cold and they become full of plants. Sweep and tidy floors, sand and oil benches and gently wash glass or plastic film with water and a soft brush or spray gun.

12

After harvesting from vegetable beds, any areas of bare soil should be planted with a winter crop, mulched with compost or sown with a green manure. This will protect the soil from weather damage, ensuring it is in good health for next year's growing (see page 168).

Celebrate the season

Although high summer has passed and autumn is approaching, I always feel that this is the time of year when summer is at its most vibrant. Residual heat from the sun has built up and the sea has warmed to levels that encourage a dip (even here in the UK!). Hiking, wild swimming and other outdoor activities are on the agenda, while the possibility of spotting rare stag beetles, water voles, hummingbird hawk moths and other summer visitors increases. As fruit, nuts and berries ripen in the hedgerows, the local wildlife makes the most of this bountiful time, and avian visitors such as swallows and house martins line up on overhead power lines, passing the time before they depart for distant lands.

Harvest and forage

Late summer sees an abundance of berries and currants, most of which are relatively easy to grow.

Although hedgerows can provide blackberries, garden varieties can give improved fruit size and flavour. Blackberries 'Chester' and 'Oregon Thornless' crop vigorously and helpfully lack the sharp thorns of their native cousins. For raspberries, 'Autumn Bliss' is a must, though for an unusual gold colour I also grow 'Alpengold'.

For me, there is nothing quite like homemade blackcurrant jelly on toast, and red and white currants are great for adding to jams and desserts where their aromatic, sharp flavour helps to balance any sweetness. Redcurrant 'Rovada' and blackcurrant 'Ben Sarek' are perfect for growing in containers, while blackcurrant 'Ben Hope' produces a delicious crop, even on poor soils. All can be grown as bushes, though red and white currants can be trained into fans or cordons, making them incredibly decorative and compact.

Blueberries are another easy crop and lend themselves to container cultivation where you can ensure they have the acidic, moist conditions they enjoy. Potting with ericaceous compost, watering with rainwater and feeding with a liquid feed for acid-loving plants once a month will keep them in top health. All blueberries crop over an extended period of time, although early varieties such as 'Bluecrop' work well with later cropping varieties like 'Bluegold'. 'Chandler' has large fruit on a relatively compact plant, while 'Pink Lemonade' ripens to an attractive pink colour. It's worth growing two or three varieties as this will improve pollination, ensuring you have more fruit over a longer picking season.

A home for nature

While our gardens are spaces for us to enjoy the plants we grow, they are also there to support wildlife. Having a variety of bugs, birds, amphibians and mammals living in your garden not only helps them, but also works to create a diverse and healthy ecosystem that promotes balance in the garden and prevents any extreme pest problems.

Though it's important to provide habitat throughout the year, late summer is when many insects and animals begin to look for places to spend the winter. By making a few simple additions to your garden, you can encourage as many visitors as possible.

A humble log and stick pile may not seem like an important feature of your garden, however it's akin to the fallen dead branches that you would find in a woodland. The decaying wood provides food for bugs and fungi, as well as a home for mosses, lichens and all sorts of wildlife. To create the habitat pile, stack and pile a mixture of twigs and logs (with the bark still attached) in a quiet, part-shaded corner of the garden. Ensure the pile has direct contact with the soil to help the fungi, plants and bugs to quickly colonise.

To develop your log pile further, add pockets of soft material such as grass clippings, herbaceous perennial cuttings and fallen leaves. This will encourage a wider range of wildlife such as hedgehogs and slow worms that will enjoy the insulative properties of the pile throughout the cold winter months.

Going further still, you can create dead hedges or walls, either by stacking logs or using branches, twigs and debris woven between upright supportive stakes that have been driven into the ground. They can be made to look quite attractive and provide interesting structure and shape to your garden, while crucially offering all the benefits of a habitat pile.

A bug hotel is a compact way of providing a home for invertebrates including insects like ladybirds, lacewings and solitary bees. There are many bug hotels available to buy, although it can be fun to construct a version of your own. Use twigs, canes, pebbles and natural materials, along with old slabs, broken pots and roof tiles to create a variety of different dry spaces that bugs can shelter in.

A bee hotel is very similar to a bug hotel, although as the name suggests it is for solitary bees and focuses on creating holes or hollow tubes for the bees to lay their eggs into. These can be purchased or simply made using some old timber and log offcuts, chopped bamboo canes and dried hollow plant stems. Arrange the various items within a supportive frame. This can then be attached to a wall, fence or tree, somewhere bright, sunny and sheltered. Do note that bee hotels need to be cleaned or replaced each year, so do a little research before you start.

A pond is an excellent way to provide a habitat for wildlife (see page 74). Not only will it provide a water source throughout the year, it also offers a home for many amphibians and invertebrates that hibernate in water during the winter or use water to reproduce. There are many different shapes and sizes to choose from, although for wildlife the key is to make it deep enough so as not to freeze (that's a minimum of 60cm). It's also vital to have different depth levels and to include aquatic and marginal plants.

Late summer

Hedgerow liqueur

Trees and bushes are a living larder of food and many of the wild and seasonal fruits you'll find at this time of year lend themselves to flavouring alcohol. Their sharp taste can be sweetened with sugar to make a delicious liqueur that can be enjoyed on its own or used in cocktails.

A traditional hedgerow fruit commonly used for infusing in spirits is the sloe, which can be found from late summer into autumn in thickets of shrubby blackthorn. The numerous fruits develop from ivory blossom in spring and have a distinct appearance: dark purple, almost black spherical balls approximately 15mm in diameter and covered in a greyish bloom. The flesh is pale green and has a tart, acerbic flavour that is softened and sweetened when infused in alcohol.

Blackberries and raspberries are a good alternative to sloes and faster to flavour the spirit. Using these sweet fruits in an infusion means adding less sugar, which makes the end result more of a spirit than a liqueur.

For a more rustic approach, try using a range of berries, mixing sloes with rosehips, hawberries and elderberries. The result is a complex flavour with many warming notes; perfect poured over ice and enjoyed as a little autumn pick-me-up.

Whichever fruit you use – and whether you choose brandy, gin, vodka or whisky as a base – the method is roughly the same. After foraging, the fruit should be washed thoroughly. For most fruits, it's important to break the skin to allow the flavours to fully infuse the spirit – this can be done by pricking, crushing or slicing the fruit, though an easier option is to freeze it. Freezing not only breaks the skins, but in the case of sloes and rosehips, it can sweeten the flavour too.

You'll need about 300–400g of fruit for every 75cl of spirit. Place into a large, sterilised preserving jar and add about 60g of sugar. Shake the jar every couple of days until the sugar is dissolved and then store to allow the fruit to infuse the spirit. Depending on the fruit, this can take anything from four weeks (raspberries) to 12 weeks (sloes). When ready, taste to see if more time or sugar is required. If not, filter through a fine sieve or muslin before bottling and enjoying.

Autumn

Early autumn

The autumn equinox marks the end of astronomical summer and, as the days gradually shorten, this time of year feels like a gentle saunter into a new season. In the mornings, heavy dew gathers on plants and garden structures, which twinkle like gems as the sun rises. Bejewelled spiders' webs hang from glistening leaves and twigs, and spangled flowers, berries and hips gently nod under the weight of their temporary embellishment. The soft light of the early sun brings everything to life and it's a moment in the garden to just look and marvel.

These magical mornings are a direct response to a change in the seasons: as the nights become longer and cooler, the drop in air temperature causes condensation to form. This change also affects the plants, as deciduous species prepare to lose their leaves and begin to change from their green summer garb to the many shades of yellow, orange and red associated with autumn.

For wildlife there is still time to prepare, and it's now that I pay particular notice to the butterflies and bees visiting the early autumn flowers. Everything from red admirals and commas to bumblebees and honey bees are feeding before they find somewhere sheltered to begin their long sleep. House martins and swifts dart through the insect-rich sky fuelling up before their migrations.

Despite the cooling temperatures, the sunny days bring enough warmth to ripen fruit and vegetables, as well as to encourage the production of flowers. Daisies open in vibrant shades of pink and yellow, matched by the range of ornamental salvias and late-season annuals. Soon the leaves will join in this carnival of colour and nature's final hurrah before the cold of winter sets in.

Plants in season

By early autumn we're nearing the final stretch of the floral race, sprinting towards the finish line with vibrant displays from perennials such as asters, persicaria and rudbeckia. Hydrangea heads respond to the lowering temperatures with a change in colour, while scented shrubs like *Heptacodium miconioides* (seven son flower tree) are triggered into flowering. Not to be outdone, however, crab apples, hawthorns and roses present their ripening fruit just as the first deciduous leaves of the *Cercidiphyllum japonicum* (katsura tree) begin to colour and fall to create a sugary candyfloss-scented carpet.

Althaea cannabina →
PALM-LEAF MARSH MALLOW

A beautiful mallow with sturdy stems that gracefully reach high to hold masses of candy-pink, bell-shaped flowers with dark centres. From a distance, they appear to almost float. Great in naturalistic and mixed borders, and equally suitable for a gravel garden, this herbaceous perennial is best planted in a sunny position. Avoid soil that sits wet in winter and exposed sites, and employ the Chelsea chop (see page 96) in May to prevent tall stems from flopping. Purchase container-grown plants throughout the year, or sow seeds direct in summer or indoors in spring. *Fully hardy throughout the UK (RHS H7, USDA 6a-1). H x S: 2.5 x 1m.*

Calamagrostis brachytricha →

Thin, glossy leaves form a dense tussock through spring and summer, followed by beautiful opalescent plumes that reach out and catch the autumn light. Both foliage and seedheads continue into the winter, turning a sandy colour. Beautiful in a mixed perennial border where it will quietly remain in the background until the arrival of autumn when it becomes the star. Prefers a sunny position and a rich, free-draining soil, though it will cope with light shade and heavier soils. Purchase and plant in late summer or spring, or divide existing clumps in winter or early spring. *Hardy throughout most of the UK (RHS H6, USDA 6b/7a). H x S: 1.3m x 90cm.*

Cotinus 'Grace' →

SMOKE BUSH 'GRACE'

A vigorous, deciduous shrub with large leaves that are a deep burgundy through the growing season, turning shades of vibrant orange and scarlet in autumn. During summer, lightly pruned specimens will put out delicate panicles of tiny flowers that from a distance give the impression of smoke. Note that hard pruning will result in vigorous regrowth and more foliage. Ideal for adding colour and seasonal structure to a shrub or mixed border. Plant in full sun to light shade in any reasonable soil. Purchase container-grown plants throughout the year, but avoid planting in the heat of midsummer. *Hardy throughout most of the UK (RHS H5, USDA 7b/8a). H x S: 4 x 4m.*

Early autumn

Crataegus persimilis 'Prunifolia' ↑
BROAD-LEAVED COCKSPUR THORN

A small, deciduous, hardy tree with a broad canopy that's perfect for compact gardens. Spring gives way to fresh glossy leaves that are quickly followed by clusters of small white flowers. The leaves remain green through summer before turning shades of orange and crimson in autumn. The generous fruit also turns a vivid red and persists on the stems long after leaf fall, making this tree a seasonal focal point. Best in full sun, it can also take a little shade. Purchase grafted trees from late winter to early spring and plant in any reasonable soil that's mulched with organic matter. *Fully hardy throughout the UK (RHS H7, USDA 6a-1). H x S: 8 x 7m.*

Dahlia 'Sarah Raven' ↑
DAHLIA 'SARAH RAVEN'

Dahlias are a fantastic and vast group of plants that come in many forms and colours, flowering their socks off from midsummer until the first frosts. 'Sarah Raven' is an anemone type with a dark red centre that's surrounded by loose petals of intense scarlet, burgundy and orange. A great addition to a border, container or cutting patch that's in a sunny spot with rich, moist but free-draining soil. Plant out from tubers or cuttings after the risk of frost has passed, though in mild areas you can leave tubers in the ground and protect with a deep mulch. *Half-hardy requiring winter protection in all but the mildest parts of the UK (RHS H3, USDA 9b/10a). H x S: 90 x 60cm.*

Heliopsis helianthoides var. *scabra* 'Bleeding Hearts' →
FALSE SUNFLOWER 'BLEEDING HEARTS'

A choice perennial with dark green, healthy foliage that appears in spring as a clump and is attractively flushed with burgundy tints. Growing taller in summer, the dark stems display the vibrant reddish orange flowers, which appear en masse during late summer and early autumn. Great for mixed herbaceous borders, large containers or the cutting patch. For the best performance grow in full sun in a sheltered position in moisture-retentive, free-draining soil. Buy container-grown plants and plant in spring or summer. *Hardy throughout most of the UK (RHS H4, USDA 8b/9a). H x S: 1.2m x 50cm.*

Hylotelephium 'Red Cauli' →
STONECROP 'RED CAULI'

A vibrant perennial with architectural, succulent-like stems and foliage that is burgundy throughout the growing season. It forms a loose clump before flowering in late summer and early autumn with tight cushions or terminal clusters of vibrant cherry red flowers. A good choice for the front of a border, gravel garden or cutting patch. Plant container-bought plants or divide in spring and summer. Take cuttings in late spring. Prefers a warm sunny site in any reasonable, free-draining soil. *Fully hardy throughout the UK (RHS H7, USDA 10b). H x S: 50 x 50cm.*

Early autumn

Rosa glauca →
RED-LEAVED ROSE

A wild-looking species rose with long, arching branches that hold the simple grey-purple foliage from early spring until leaf fall in autumn. Beginning early summer, small pink flowers with white eyes appear along the stems, complementing the foliage. As autumn arrives, subtle red hips become more conspicuous and persist into winter. Perfect for a shrub or mixed border, meadow or naturalistic planting. Grow in full sun for the best foliage and flowers, and in any reasonable soil. Plant bare-root plants in winter or container-grown plants in spring. *Fully hardy throughout the UK (RHS H7, USDA 6a-1). H x S: 2.5 x 2.5m.*

Salvia 'Amistad'
SAGE 'AMISTAD'

A superb border salvia that has vigour through the year, with verdant, scented, nettle-like foliage that forms a healthy, upright bush. From late summer to early autumn, spires of the deepest purple flowers appear, held to the stems with attractive contrasting blackcurrant calyces. A perfect plant for a mixed border or large container. Best planted in a warm, sheltered site, it prefers full sun and fertile, free-draining soil. Purchase and plant pot-grown specimens in late spring, or take cuttings in late summer for planting the following year. *Half-hardy requiring winter protection in all but the mildest parts of the UK (RHS H3, USDA 9b/10a). H x S: 1.5m x 50cm.*

Symphyotrichum 'Little Carlow' →
ASTER 'LITTLE CARLOW'

A well-behaved perennial aster with masses of joyful, violet-blue daisies with yellow centres held on thin, upright stems during late summer and early autumn. The plant appears from the soil in spring to form a mound of attractive dark foliage, before rising with leafy stems from which the flowers appear. Good for mixed herbaceous borders, naturalistic planting or a cutting bed. Best planted in a sunny spot in any reasonable soil. Purchase container-grown plants throughout the year and plant in spring or late summer. *Fully hardy throughout the UK (RHS H7, USDA 6a-1). H x S: 90 x 50cm.*

Tithonia rotundifolia →
MEXICAN SUNFLOWER

A tender but vigorous branching annual with fresh green leaves and strong stems that race skywards to hold masses of large, orange, daisy-like flowers that will easily compete with any surrounding late summer and autumn colour. Continue to deadhead to ensure flowering right up until the first frost. A lovely annual addition to mixed borders, tropical planting schemes, large containers and the cutting patch. Best grown in rich, free-draining soil in full sun. Grow from seed in spring and plant out after the last frosts. *Avoid frost as tender throughout the UK (RHS H2, USDA 11-13). H x S: 2m x 50cm.*

Verbena bonariensis →
PURPLE TOP

Standing to guard, this upright perennial has a small, basal cluster of semi-evergreen leaves from which rise angular stems that branch to hold groups of small, glowing purple flowers from midsummer to the first frost. Very attractive in an open border, gravel garden or left to seed along path edges. Plant in a warm, sunny position in any free-draining soil – wet, cold winters may cause it to suffer. Purchase container-grown plants throughout the year, sow seed in early spring and plant in spring to summer. *Hardy throughout most of the UK (RHS H4, USDA 8b/9a). H x S: 1.5m x 50cm.*

Plants in season

Early autumn

Things to do

Sow a wildflower patch

Early autumn is a time when many plants set seed in preparation for next year's growing season. This is true for wildflower species and so now is the perfect time to be in tune with the natural rhythm of the plants and to create your own wildflower patch. You could simply leave an area of your lawn unmown (it will demonstrate just how diverse these spaces can be), though if you want more flowers and a longer season of interest, all you need is a little elbow grease and enthusiasm.

1   Identify your soil type and site aspect and select plant varieties that best suit the conditions. Some species, such as *Leucanthemum vulgare* (ox-eye daisy), are fairly adaptable, while others, such as *Filipendula ulmaria* (meadowsweet) and *Teucrium scorodonia* (wood sage), may require more specific conditions. There are many websites that specialise in fresh, sustainable wildflower seeds and sell mixes for specific conditions.

2   Like painting a picture, it's important to have a good quality canvas for your wildflower patch. Mark out the selected area: this could be a geometric shape or curved organic swathe, but aim for a minimum size of 50cm x 1m. Begin by weeding out any vigorous, tall and pernicious weeds such as young brambles, nettles and docks. Then cut the grass short and collect and remove the clippings.

3   To prepare the site for sowing, you need to open and weaken the existing grass sward (the top layer of grass-covered soil). To do this, heavily scarify or scratch the sward using a scarifying machine or spring-tine rake. This removes the layer of built-up detritus and scratches away surface roots, creating spaces for the seeds to fall into and make direct contact with the soil. The seed can then be sown direct into the area; alternatively, you can sow seed into plug trays and plant out later as little plants.

4   The wildflower patch should be cut at least once a year, but you can mow it more frequently, depending on the season of interest of your wildflowers. The grass and flowers should be cut in late summer or early autumn and allowed to dry and shed seed before you rake up and remove the debris.

PAGE 141 Aconitum and persicaria provide valuable late-season colour and make good bedfellows as they like similar growing conditions OPPOSITE *Leucanthemum vulgare* (ox-eye daisy) and *Anthriscus sylvestris* (cow parsley) provide a quintessential look for a wildflower patch in late spring and early summer

Early autumn

This helps prevent the soil fertility from improving and encourages the wildflowers to self-seed.

5   If you find the grass is too vigorous and out-competing the flowers, then a parasitic plant called *Rhinanthus minor* (yellow rattle) can help: it reduces grass growth and allows more space for the flowers to establish. You can also experiment and extend the flower display by adding in naturalistic perennials like *Liatris pycnostachya* (prairie blazing star) and *Veronicastrum virginicum* 'Erica' (culver's root 'Erica') or bulbs such as *Gladiolus communis* subsp. *byzantinus* (byzantine gladiolus) and *Ornithogalum ponticum* 'Sochi'.

Look after your lawn

While not being the most biologically diverse part of a garden, a lawn can be a key feature, working practically as a soft, green space for kids and pets to play or as a breathing space to relax and enjoy views of the garden. Historically, lawns have been maintained as pristine green spaces, but luckily this rigid approach has relaxed. Whatever the shape and size of your lawn, there are a few tricks to making sure it stays healthy and fit for purpose.

Many people are under the misconception that a lawn is low maintenance. In reality, it requires mowing every week or two during the growing season to keep it in good condition. The edges should also be trimmed to prevent them invading paths and borders, which if neglected can cause more maintenance problems.

Scarifying is a worthwhile exercise. If you have a large lawn, it's easy to hire a scarifier machine that does most of the hard work. If the area is small, a spring-tine rake will do. Scarifying pulls out thatch, which is the dead plant material that can create a barrier that impedes the percolation of water. Scarifying also encourages the grass to grow more upright and thick, rather than flat along the surface.

With regular use your lawn may suffer compaction, which hinders drainage and

creates an unhealthy environment for the soil organisms and grass to thrive. The simplest way to alleviate this is to use a digging fork to spike the ground or gently lever and lift it slightly around the compacted area. Another effective method is to use a specialist tine lawn aerator tool or machine that removes cylindrical plugs from the ground. These plugs should be left on the surface to dry and then broken up using a mower, scarifier or rake. Some of the soil will make it back into the holes, but it will be loose and contain air, which will alleviate the compaction.

After the maintenance outlined here, you may wish to over-sow the lawn with seed. Mix the seed with topsoil before applying to the ground, as this improves the germination rate, giving the seed something easy to root into. Patches of turf can also be bought and used to repair damaged areas. Make sure the patch sits level and its edges are tightly enclosed with the surrounding lawn. Fill any gaps with firmed topsoil. Watering with a homemade liquid feed (see page 43) can also help any weak grass growth.

Unless you have a bowling green or golf course, your approach to lawn maintenance can be relaxed. It is not good practice to apply chemical feeds and weedkillers, and meticulously hand weeding can be laborious. Instead, welcome the odd patch of clover, dandelions or buttercups and know that the wildlife will thank you for it.

Early autumn

Harvest and store produce

One of the highlights of being a gardener is bringing in a harvest. There is something so satisfying about seeing, smelling and tasting the produce that you have lovingly tended. When ready, a gentle twist will see most crops depart from the soil or the parent plant, however secateurs may be required for tougher stems such as beans and squashes. Harvesting can take place throughout the year, depending on your crop, although early autumn is a busy time and it is important to store your produce correctly.

Many root vegetables, including beetroots, carrots and parsnips, can be left in the ground and stored there through winter, ready to pull up when needed. Potatoes and Jerusalem artichokes fall into this category, but they should have their tops removed first. If, like me, you have a problem with ground (keel) slugs or live in an area with freezing conditions, then crops should be lifted now and stored in boxes of soil or sand. A traditional option is a clamp – a nest of straw that holds the vegetables, which is then covered in soil.

Although aubergines, cucumbers, tomatoes and peppers are always slow to get going, they soon gain pace and growers are often left with a glut in late summer and early autumn. Thankfully there are many ways to preserve them. Cucumbers can be pickled, while the others can be dry roasted and stored in jars filled with oil. Alternatively, cook down with fresh herbs to make a sauce that can be frozen for later use.

You'll know your squash is ready to harvest when the skin is firm and true to colour, with the stem showing signs of drying. Winter squashes need to be cured after harvesting, a process that lets the sun dry and harden the skins, which can improve the flavour. Leave to cure on a sunny windowsill for a week or two. Once cured, they can be stored somewhere cool and dry or left on a shelf (they look beautiful and keep for months).

Harvest onions and garlic when the bulbs are firm and the foliage has turned yellow, folded over or started to die back, then trim off the roots. These also need to be cured: leave on trays or in boxes somewhere cool and dry. When the skins are papery, store in a dry, cool, frost-free environment. I find that onions and garlic always get used, but if you want to store them for longer, try pickling small onions and smoking garlic bulbs.

Peas, beans and mangetout always come in gluts. Fresh peas can go straight in the freezer. Broad beans, runner beans and French beans will freeze better if they are first blanched in hot water for a couple of minutes. Borlotti, orca and French beans can be dried, then shelled and stored in an airtight jar.

Task list

Jobs to do during early autumn

1

Sow annual herbs such as basil, coriander and chervil and grow these indoors for a fresh supply during early winter. Individual plants of parsley and mint can also be lifted from the garden, potted up and brought inside to give you a supply of fresh herbs going into autumn.

2

Before the worst of the weather arrives, cut and dry flowers and seedheads collected from the garden and the wild for use indoors (see pages 103 and 154). Hydrangea heads capture autumnal tones as they dry, while teasels and eryngiums work well in winter arrangements and wreaths.

3

Cut back and remove early-flowering annuals from borders and cutting beds that have produced seed. This may include cornflowers, nigella and sweet peas. With these, as with many other plants, you can save seed for growing again next year (see page 114).

4

Many annual herbs will be coming to an end now and so it is a good idea to harvest and dry some for winter. Cut and wash the freshest tips before leaving to dry in a paper bag or on a tray inside. After a couple of weeks, when fully dry, remove woody stems and then crumble, before storing in a jar or airtight container.

5

Plant out hardy salad varieties that were sown in late summer, including mustards, rocket and winter lettuce, along with spring greens. The plants should establish quickly, but keep a watchful eye for slug damage while they are still young. As temperatures drop, protect the crops with horticultural fleece, a growing tunnel or cloche.

6

Vigorous brassicas such as flower sprouts and purple spouting broccoli will have grown large and tall through the summer months. It's worth offering these plants some support before the inclement weather arrives, staking with a cane and tying in with string to prevent strong winds and rain from knocking down these gentle giants.

Things to do

7

At this time of year, growth in the garden slows and time spent on routine tasks reduces. Now is the moment to plan for next year and beyond, thinking about any developments involving hard landscaping, building or structural maintenance. Organise for these jobs to be completed during the dormant period so that when spring arrives, the plants can grow uninterrupted.

8

Keep an eye out for problems with box hedging and topiary, as both blight and box moth caterpillar are prevalent at this time of year. For blight, spray with a Top Buxus health mix or alternative fungicide. For the box moth caterpillar, apply the natural bacterium *Bacillus thuringiensis*. Always double check the manufacturer's guidelines when using any biocide.

9

If you have leaf mould piles (see pages 168 and 175) now is a good time to make use of them before this year's leaves fall and need collecting. Scrape away the top, dry layer to hopefully reveal some rich, dark brown leaf litter. This is perfect for incorporating into borders or vegetable beds, but can also be used to mulch permanent container planting or enrich a soil-based potting mix.

10

Make preparations for winter by cleaning bird feeders and bird baths. As the weather turns cool, clean feeders regularly with a diluted disinfectant to maintain a healthy environment and prevent bacterial growth. Top up feeders with a good quality seed through autumn and winter when the birds need it most.

11

Prick out and pot on hardy annual and biennial seedlings that were sown in late summer. These will continue to grow and develop their roots for another couple of months and can then be planted out before winter or kept somewhere sheltered outside ready to be planted in early spring.

12

As nights become cooler, move houseplants indoors and tender plants undercover inside or in a greenhouse. They will be entering a dormant period soon, so won't require feeding or repotting, but a thorough tidy and weed is welcome, as well as inspection for any pests like red spider mite or slugs.

Early autumn

Celebrate the season

Though early autumn can still hold summer's warmth and bounty, the air feels different: once lightly perfumed with the scent of summer flowers, there is now the earthy, sweet smell of senescence, as leaves and berries start to fall and the fruiting bodies of fungi appear.

This season has ancient associations with harvests, and festivals around the world celebrate the gathering of crops along with the perpetuity and promise of the next growing season. From *Homowo* in Ghana to *Chuseok* in Korea, events encourage people to share the abundance of food.

For me, it's also a moment to take stock, not just in the garden, but also at home. I like to organise and prepare the house for evenings indoors and this is the time that natural objet d'art found on walks begin to collect on a nature table or in a bowl, reinforcing a connection with the outdoors.

Harvest and forage

Early autumn sees the garden fill with the smell of ripening apples, mostly from the windfalls that litter the paths and go on to feed the blackbirds and fieldfares later in the year. Despite this, there are always lots of apples to pick and store in cardboard trays, and plenty to juice for cider, cook in crumbles and slice and dry for the larder. Whatever outdoor space you have, there is an apple tree that will suit.

For the larger garden, cider and cookers are an option; you will also need a fair amount of space to grow dessert apples like 'Blenheim Orange', as these trees reach a good size. These types can be grown as standards (lollypop-shaped and branching at a height of about 1.2m) or large trees. Both should be pruned in the traditional manner in winter. For small spaces, a low, horizontal stepover or thin, vertical cordon form is more suitable – the size of the tree is restricted by a dwarfing rootstock and can be maintained through summer pruning. Dessert varieties such as 'Falstaff' and 'Laxton's Fortune' are good options, providing they are grafted on to dwarfing rootstocks. Whatever size or form you choose, make sure it is self-fertile (will pollinate itself) or has another tree close by that is in the same pollination or flowering group. This ensures that the flowers will be successfully fertilised and produce fruit.

Peppers are another late crop that are super useful in the kitchen and decorative while growing. From a late-spring sowing, they will happily grow in a pot on a windowsill or sunny terrace and begin cropping in midsummer. They come in all sorts of colours and vary considerably in flavour and heat. 'Doux des Landes' and 'Marconi Rosso' are both reliable sweet peppers, while 'Chocolate Habanero', 'Piment de Bresse' and 'Lemon Drop' are chilli types that pack more heat.

Create a harvest wreath

Traditionally wreaths have a strong association with winter and festive celebrations, however they are beautiful in any season and can encapsulate what the natural world has to offer. As autumn arrives, there is a wealth of foliage and flower colour, along with berries and hips, nuts and seedpods to work with. Your wreath can be simple, using just one or two repeating items for a dramatic effect, or it can be complex and asymmetric.

1 Think ahead and collect foliage, cones, seedheads, hips, berries and flowers on dry days before leaving them to dry fully. Damp and dirty materials can promote mould.

2 Form a circular frame using pliable twigs: willow, lime and dogwoods with colourful stems work well. Begin by tying two twigs together at one end and then weave together the other ends to form a circle. Add more twigs, starting at different points around the ring to strengthen and help hold the shape. A quick, easy and reusable alternative is a wire or rattan frame, which can be bought online or in florist shops.

3 Now add the base foliage. Here I've used dried bracken and purple beech stems. I've used cotton string to secure these elements to the frame. Start at one point and work around the wreath until it is fully covered. Alternatively, leave some of it naked for an asymmetric shape. The attached foliage should provide you with a nest of materials into which you can weave other items.

4 Next, add the main decorative elements, particularly anything that may be heavy. This could be contrasting foliage, ornate twigs and seedpods, but may also include large rosehips, crab apples, conkers or cobnuts. Here I've used horse chestnut casings that had to be individually fixed to the wreath using florists' wire.

5 Before completing the wreath, fix on a method of attachment. It could be as simple and discrete as a string loop or wire hoop. Alternatively, you may choose to make a feature of it with coloured ribbon or decorative string.

6 The final stage is to embellish the wreath with small, delicate details such as dried flowers, small rosehips, little cones and anything else you've found outdoors. I like to do this when the wreath is already hanging in position so I can see how it will look once finished.

Celebrate the season

Early autumn

Attend a fungal foray

Fungi grow throughout the year as microscopic fungal hyphae, though they usually only become apparent when they produce the fruiting bodies that we recognise as mushrooms and toadstools. The heavy dew and mild damp days of early autumn are perfect conditions for them to flourish. As with all foraging, there is so much to learn: regardless of which mushrooms you find, you'll come back with an improved understanding and appreciation of how important these organisms are to our planet.

The variety of mushrooms and toadstools is vast. While differing visually, they can also be identified by spore colour, habitat, scent and growth habit. The difference between two species can be minor and the consequences of getting it wrong (and consuming something you think is edible) can be fatal. If you're a newcomer to fungi foraging, it's important to make your first trips out with someone experienced and to develop the right skills before going it alone. Many wildlife organisations, country parks and foraging schools offer foray days where you can learn how to forage safely. The British Mycological Society is a good starting point for more information.

Typical equipment includes a basket or cardboard box, along with paper bags that are useful for storing the mushrooms – avoid plastic or metal as these can make the fungi sweat. Other bits of kit include a comprehensive field guide, a pencil and notepad, and a smartphone or camera – a hand lens with at least 10x magnification is particularly useful.

Fungi have adapted to grow in all manner of situations: deciduous and coniferous forests can host an impressive range of mushrooms, along with meadows, parks and moorland. Foraging in some areas is prohibited and so always check before you set out.

Back at home, store your bounty in a breathable container in the fridge or somewhere cool; they should last for several days. I like them sautéed with a little butter and black pepper on a slice of sourdough so you can really taste their unique flavour. A great way to preserve mushrooms is to dry them. Brush them clean, then slice them before placing in a dehydrator or on a tray and into an oven set at the lowest temperature. Check on them regularly, and once completely dry, store in an airtight container.

Early autumn

Late autumn

Under late autumn's grey skies burnished leaves fall to the ground, rustling underfoot and fluttering along on gusts of wind. Boots, heavy knits and waterproof jackets are back in service and ready to help tackle the changeable weather that this season can bring.

Despite the darker days and longer nights, late autumn can be a colourful time in the garden. Crab apples, rosehips and berries hang brightly, while carpets of golden and russet orange leaves congregate on the ground in the garden and the wild. Bark and stem colours begin to become prominent, especially when lit by the glowing setting sun. Herbaceous perennials are making a swift retreat below the earth, leaving their skeletal stems to face the winter storms. Deciduous trees and shrubs finish their preparations, discarding the last soft leaves, while the evergreens stand fast, lending important green structure that can offer shelter to garden birds, mammals and insects.

There is plenty going on in the garden and even on the dullest of days I am kept busy and motivated. It's now that the autumn tidy judiciously begins, though I'm careful to leave areas untouched for wildlife. Vegetables are harvested, stored and checked, with only those below ground, or tough enough to withstand winter, left outside. As always there is preparation for the future: pruning, lifting and dividing, as well as the planting of spring bulbs that will burst forth with enthusiasm as the new growing season begins next year.

There is much to do, so grab a rake, secateurs and your gardening gloves and venture outside to be part of this amazing seasonal journey.

Plants in season

Late autumn sees evergreen plants come into their own, including most conifers and rhododendrons, as well as shrubs such as *Lonicera pileata* (box-leaved honeysuckle), *Osmanthus* × *burkwoodii* (Burkwood osmanthus) and *Viburnum davidii* (David viburnum). Whether clipped to a sculptural form or left shaggy and loose, their defiant foliage stands solid in pleasing contrast to the light tracery of leafless deciduous species. Ornamental grasses rise to the occasion too, with *Miscanthus sinensis* (eulalia) cultivars turning shades of soft orange and red, while molinia species glow golden. Late-flowering *Actaea simplex* 'Brunette' (baneberry 'Brunette'), *Hesperantha coccinea* (crimson flag lily) and *Symphyotrichum cordifolium* 'Elegans' (aster 'Elegans') offer bursts of colour and a nectar source for bees and butterflies.

Acer japonicum 'Aconitifolium' →
DOWNY JAPANESE MAPLE
'ACONITIFOLIUM'

A choice Japanese maple with beautifully lobed palmate foliage resembling those of aconitum. Emerging green in spring, the young leaves are accompanied by small red flowers that hang downwards. By autumn the leaves turn brilliant shades of scarlet and crimson, before falling to the ground. Slow growing with a neat habit, this acer makes a perfect addition to a small garden or a focal point within a larger space. Plant in full sun to light shade, protecting the tree from drying winds. It's happy in all but the heaviest, wettest soils. Buy and plant grafted trees in early spring or late summer; bare-root stock may be available for planting during winter. *Hardy throughout most of the UK (RHS H6, USDA 6b/7a). H x S: 7 x 5m.*

← *Anisodontea* 'El Rayo'
AFRICAN MALLOW 'EL RAYO'

A superb, semi-evergreen perennial sub-shrub that flowers in nearly every month of the year. Thin, woody, cinnamon-coloured stems hold three-lobed maple-like leaves, while bright pink flowers appear singularly along the upper stems from leaf axils. A slightly tender plant, it's best given a warm, sunny and sheltered spot and it will look great in a container, naturalistic border or gravel garden. Plant in free-draining soil, avoiding any winter wet and excessive cold. Purchase and plant container-grown plants during late spring and early summer; take semi-ripe cuttings in late summer (see page 116). *Half-hardy requiring winter protection in all but the mildest parts of the UK (RHS H3, USDA 9b/10a). H x S: 1.5 x 1m.*

← *Bergenia ciliata*
FRINGED ELEPHANT'S EARS

A dramatic foliage plant with large, rounded leaves that are covered in silvery hairs that persist into the coldest months, eventually succumbing to heavy frost. The younger, smaller leaves flushed with red remain untouched and will begin growing larger in spring, when clear pink, bell-like flowers hang from stout stems. A statement for the front of a border or container, it is best grown in moist but free-draining soil in sun or part shade. Purchase container-grown plants or divide and take rhizome cuttings in spring. *Hardy throughout most of the UK (RHS H4, USDA 8b/9a). H x S: 40 x 50cm.*

Late autumn

Ceratostigma willmottianum ↑
CHINESE PLUMBAGO

A small, reliable deciduous shrub that forms an increasing mound of fresh green leaves from spring into summer. It comes alive during late summer, when numerous electric blue flowers appear in terminal clusters. Accompanied by autumnal foliage, it makes quite a show for late autumn and continues into winter with tufted, ornamental seedheads.

Great for a mixed border, parterre or large container. It is best grown in full sun to part shade in soil that doesn't become waterlogged. Purchase container-grown plants and plant in spring or summer, avoiding the hottest months. *Hardy throughout most of the UK (RHS H4, USDA 8b/9a H x S: 1.2 x 1.2m.*

Cercidiphyllum japonicum ↑
KATSURA TREE

An upright deciduous tree that matures to a broad canopy and is famed for its sweet, burnt-sugar scent that develops when the leaves are frosted and fall. Reddish buds and inconspicuous flowers give way to young, rounded, heart-shaped leaves, which have a bronze tint that fades to green as they age. In autumn, the foliage turns warm shades of buttery yellow and apricot, before falling as the frosts arrive. A lovely tree for a focal point in a lawn or by a driveway. Best in full sun or light shade, in a moisture-retentive, free-draining soil. Purchase and plant trees from late autumn to early spring. *Hardy throughout most of the UK (RHS H5, USDA 7b/8a). H x S: 10 x 6m.*

Hakonechloa macra →
JAPANESE FOREST GRASS

An accommodating perennial grass that has something to offer in nearly every season. Verdant, tufty growth appears in spring, extending up and out to create a soft mound of tactile foliage that ripples in the breeze. Light panicles appear late summer, before the foliage turns golden in autumn and then buff in early winter, maintaining its interest and shape until early spring. Happy in sun to full shade in any moisture-retentive soil. Purchase plants during the growing season or divide in spring. *Fully hardy throughout the UK (RHS H7, USDA 6a-1). H x S: 50 x 50cm.*

Ipomea lobata ↘
SPANISH FLAG

An easy-to-grow, twining climber that finds its vigour towards the latter half or the year. From seed sown in late spring, long bronze stems appear, together with exotic-looking, three-lobed leaves. From late summer, one-sided racemes of flowers emerge, moving from burnt orange to cream and giving the plant a tropical feel. As summer moves to autumn, the annual plant gathers still more vigour, continuing to flower with enthusiasm until the first frosts. It works well on obelisks in containers or over arches. Happiest in a warm, sunny spot in rich soil. Sow seed in mid-spring, grow on undercover and plant out after the risk of any late frosts has passed. *Tender, though can be grown outside in the summer in the UK (RHS H1c, USDA 11). H x S: 3 x 1m.*

Late autumn

Mespilus germanica →
COMMON MEDLAR

A deciduous, slow-growing but spreading ornamental tree with old-fashioned charm and unusual culinary fruits. Long, oval leaves appear in spring, soon followed by large, single rose-like flowers that produce the olive-brown coloured fruit that the tree is known for. In autumn the leaves turn yellow, before dropping to reveal large spherical fruits. A great talking point as well as a source of medlar for jelly. Ideal for a kitchen garden, orchard or small garden. Best in full sun in any reasonable soil. Buy and plant grafted trees in early spring or late summer. Bare-root stock may be available to plant during winter. *Hardy throughout most of the UK (RHS H6, USDA 6b/7a). H x S: 6 x 6m.*

Miscanthus nepalensis →
HIMALAYAN FAIRY GRASS

A perennial ornamental grass with silky golden tassels in early autumn that persist through winter into early spring. Foliage emerges in late spring, expanding to form an open habit, while in late summer, stems produce ornamental flowers. An elegant miscanthus that is perfect for gravel gardens or naturalistic borders. Prefers an open, sunny, but sheltered spot in free-draining soil. Sow seed in spring or buy plants during spring and summer. *Hardy throughout most of the UK (RHS H6, USDA 6b/7a). H x S: 1.2m x 60cm.*

Salvia 'Phyllis' Fancy'
SAGE 'PHYLLIS' FANCY'

A bushy, half-hardy perennial with slender, aromatic leaves throughout spring and summer. Early autumn gives rise to dark purple flower spikes with matching calyces that hold the tubular, downy white flowers that are tinted with the softest lilac. Elegant and eye-catching, the flowers continue until the first frosts. A fantastic seasonal plant for filling gaps in borders or using in containers for a late-season display. Plant in full sun in any reasonable soil. Take cuttings in late summer and overwinter indoors for planting the following spring after the frosts. *Half-hardy requiring winter protection in all but the mildest parts of the UK (RHS H3, USDA 9b/10a). H x S: 1.5 x 1m.*

Oenothera lindheimeri ↑
GAURA

A perennial that is a stalwart of the hot, sunny border where it will flower for months and months from summer right up to the first frosts. A basal cluster of lanceolate foliage gives rise to long, slender, curved stems in summer, dotted with foliage and numerous white flowers that from a distance appear to float. A worthy plant for a gravel garden or containers. Happiest in full sun and well-drained soil. Sow seed outside or take basal cuttings in spring. Alternatively, purchase and plant container-grown stock during spring and summer. *Hardy throughout most of the UK (RHS H4, USDA 8b/9a). H x S: 1.2 x 1m.*

Symphyotrichum 'Vasterival'
ASTER 'VASTERIVAL'

A soft and gently spreading hardy perennial that has masses of small, pale purple-pink daisies on willowy dark stems from late summer into autumn. In spring, soft mounds of dark green leaves slowly rise, with taller stems emerging in summer that produce flowers later in the year. A great border plant that can add romance and charm. Best in full sun in any reasonable soil. Purchase and plant container-grown stock in spring and early summer. Alternatively, divide in early spring or take cuttings in late spring. *Fully hardy throughout the UK (RHS H7, USDA 6a-1). H x S: 1.2m x 1.2m.*

Late autumn

Things to do

Look after your soil

As the growing season comes to an end, many of the regular jobs like deadheading, weeding and mowing slow down, allowing more time for larger, long-term maintenance tasks. High on the agenda should be improving soil health, which is fundamental to a garden's success. Promoting soil health is about encouraging life into the soil; everything from microorganisms to earthworms have a role to play in creating a nutritious and beneficial subterranean environment.

It is important to identify the type of soil you have as this will give you a better idea of how to manage it. In brief, soils are made up of sand, silt and clay particles in different proportions. Sandy soils are light and very free-draining, and therefore prone to leaching nutrients. Loam soils have a balance of sand, silt and clay that's ideal for good drainage and fertility. Clay soils are heavy and have poor drainage, they can hold on to nutrients so they are generally very fertile, but they are also prone to waterlogging and compaction. Soils are also affected by the bedrock they lie on and the environment around them: they can be thin, free-draining and alkaline (chalk soils) or rich, moist and acidic (those found in coniferous forests). You can test your soil for its acidity and also its texture, but simply observing what grows and how moisture behaves will tell you a lot.

Good soil health and management also reduces the risk of compaction, which occurs when soil particles are pressed together creating a dense structure that damages rooting channels and pushes out air and water, leaving an unhealthy growing environment. To prevent this, do not dig, trample or drive on soil that is wet (heavy and wet clay soil is at most risk of compaction) and see the following tips on mulch and ground cover.

Bare, weeded soil may seem tidy, but it leaves it exposed to erosion, nutrient loss and weather damage. A good way to keep soil in borders covered is to space plants so they just touch and to use ground-cover plants underneath. Two of my favourites are geraniums and *Saxifraga* × *urbium* (London pride), pictured opposite.

Mulching is a key process that will save you time and money by reducing the need for weeding and watering. To improve the structure and nutrient content of the soil, use an organic mulch that is free of weeds such as homemade compost or well-rotted manure (from an organic source to ensure it does not contain herbicides). If you wish to

only protect the soil, then a gravel or woodchip mulch will suffice.

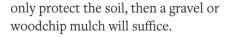

Vegetable beds can also be covered with a mulch, although you may wish to use a green manure, which can improve both soil structure and nutrient levels. Green manure is a cover crop that is sown when the soil is bare and then grows and covers the bed while not in use. When you're ready to sow or plant again, dig the green manure back into the soil. *Vicia faba* (winter field bean) and *V. sativa* (winter tares) are good green manures for heavy soils and can fix nitrogen, while *Lupinus angustifolius* (narrow-leaf lupin) performs well on light soils. *Phacelia tanacetifolia* (phacelia) is a good all-rounder – it is well behaved, easy to dig in and has lovely

flowers that are attractive to insects (pictured on page 166, top right).

During winter, fallen leaves can be left in borders to act as a mulch, although I find these can take a while to break down and may obscure early spring bulbs as well as harbour overwintering slugs. I prefer to gather the leaves to create a dedicated leaf mould pile, allowing it to rot down before using it as mulch (see pages 151 and 175).

If a soil is compacted aerate it by driving holes into it with a digging fork. For very poor-draining soils and heavily compacted subsoil it may be necessary to install French drains. However, the long-term solution is to mulch, promote soil fauna and avoid further compaction.

Plant spring bulbs

Late autumn is the time to plant spring-flowering bulbs, which are a easy way to inject additional colour and interest to the garden. While the physical act of planting a bulb (especially a few hundred) can be a little mundane, the result is far from it. Months after their autumn planting, when the memory of what was put in has almost faded to nothing, they begin to appear. I find this such an exciting time, as inevitably there is something I had completely forgotten I'd planted! One after another, the bulbs rise up to dazzle and delight with their colourful flowers, like fireworks creating lively displays and combinations for just a brief period in the gardening year.

It's worth spending a little time doing some research when choosing what bulbs to order. As with all plants, the first rule is to match the bulb with the conditions that you have. For instance, camassias prefer damper conditions than alliums and tulips, while *Anemone nemorosa* (wood anemone) is happy in shade. Unfussy bulbs for borders include early chionodoxa and hyacinths, along with later-flowering alliums and Dutch irises. You'll also find a few of my favourite bulbs in Plants in Season sections in the early and late spring chapters.

Planting times will vary depending on the bulb. Some (such as wood anemone and narcissi) prefer an early start in September, while others (such as tulips) are best planted after the first hard frosts in late autumn or early winter. As a general rule, plant the bulb to a depth that is equivalent to at least three times the height of the bulb, but always check the specific bulb as there are some exceptions. Plant the bulb root side down, pointy end up. There are bulbs that don't like to dry out and so should be planted immediately on arrival. Many of these include woodland species like erythroniums and trilliums. I like to pot these up first so I can look after them and make sure they are growing well before planting them out in the borders the following spring.

There is nothing quite as joyful as seeing a large swath of bulbs naturalising in grass. A good display can take time to establish as plants increase in numbers year-on-year by seed and offsets, but it's worth the wait. Classics include *Crocus tommasinianus* (early crocus), *Fritillaria meleagris* (snake's head fritillary) and *Camassia leichtlinii* (Californian quamash). These look brilliant interplanted with clumps of *Narcissus* 'Thalia', 'Pipit' and 'W. P. Milner'. For a natural look, I recommend mixing the bulbs together, then scattering them on the grass to plant them where they land. If grown in a lawn, allow four to five weeks after flowering for the bulb foliage to begin to die before mowing.

In terms of variety, colour, shape and size, no bulb can beat the tulip. Most tulips will often only last for a couple of years as they dislike our wet winters, so plant the bulbs in free-draining soil to get the best from them. If your soil is too heavy, then try them in raised beds or containers filled with a free-draining compost. Common advice is to add grit to the planting hole, but in my experience it won't be enough to change the soil's structure and can even act as a soakaway, draining water from the surrounding soil and exacerbating the problem.

To deter rodents or other animals from digging up your bulbs, try chicken wire set just below the surface of the soil over the bulbs, or perhaps adopt a cat. If mice are a real issue, avoid crocuses and focus on narcissi, which these rodents are generally indifferent to.

Plant a winter container

As the weather turns cold and wet, spending large amounts of time in the garden can seem less appealing. One way to maintain a positive relationship with the outside is to plant a winter container or two. These seasonal displays are excellent at providing additional interest in the garden, allowing you to flex your creativity through plant choice and arrangement. Whether you decide to venture outside or just gaze through a window from the warmth indoors, a winter container can provide uplifting joy in a season that can sometimes feel a little dark.

Select your container and consider its material: terracotta and wood have more insulative properties than metal or plastic, but terracotta can sometimes crack in severe cold if it's not frostproof. Large containers will suffer less from the cold and offer more flexibility in plant choice and arrangement than smaller ones.

I like to raise containers off the ground using pot feet, which will aid drainage and prevent freezing ground temperatures from causing damage. During the coldest months I wrap terracotta pots with hessian or burlap, which adds a natural-looking layer of additional frost protection.

Select your plants with winter in mind. Evergreen shrubs provide structure and three good choices include sarcococca

Things to do

(which produces scented white flowers through winter), *Gaultheria procumbens* (checkerberry) for its small leathery leaves and vibrant red berries, and skimmia. If you don't have enough space for a male and female skimmia, opt for *Skimmia japonica* subsp. *reevesiana* (self-fertile Japanese skimmia), which will reliably produce winter berries. All three shrubs can be purchased as small rooted cuttings. For softer elements, try the coppery foliage of *Heuchera* 'Marmalade' or the deep purple foliage of *Euphorbia amygdaloides* 'Purpurea' (wood spurge 'Purpurea'). Add texture with *Carex testacea* 'Prairie Fire' (New Zealand sedge) or *Uncinia rubra* (red hook sedge), or a clump-forming perennial like *Liriope muscari* (big blue lilyturf). Flowers can also be added: try cyclamen, hellebores and violas, as well as early spring bulbs such as *Narcissus* 'Tête-à-tête', which will come up in between your plants the following year.

Cover the container's drainage holes with a crock or two before filling with peat-free compost. Arrange the plants into a pleasing combination, then begin planting, firming the compost around the rootballs as you go. Add any bulbs that are going in. Water well to settle the compost and then periodically when conditions are dry.

In late winter you can further dress the pot, temporarily using springs of holly or variegated foliage, along with the coloured stems of dogwoods or willows.

Late autumn

Task list

Jobs to do during late autumn

1

Begin planting bulbs that you wish to force for use indoors during the festive holiday. These include *Narcissus* 'Avalanche', 'Erlicheer' and 'Zivea', along with prepared hyacinth bulbs. Bulbs should be grown in peat-free compost and placed in a warm position (see page 202).

2

Add a thick (6–8cm) layer of compost or organic mulch to no-dig vegetable beds. This will protect and feed the soil during winter, prevent any weed establishment and also ensure the beds are ready for the start of the growing season next year.

3

If you missed your chance to lift and divide plants in early spring, it's possible to do this now. Cut back the plants and then dig them up and split the rootballs using a sharp spade. Plant the younger and healthy sections, discarding the oldest central pieces.

4

If you want an extra-early crop of sweet peas, now is the time to get started. Sow seeds singularly into modules, root trainers or loo rolls – they need a deep, narrow root run. Water and keep warm indoors or in a propagator until they germinate (around ten days). Grow on with protection from the cold for a month or so, before hardening them off somewhere sheltered and free from mice (such as a cold frame). In early spring, pot on and grow on with shelter until the weather improves and they can then be planted out.

5

With the weather changing, it's time to prepare so that you are ready to protect winter salad crops when the temperatures reach freezing. Research and invest in horticultural fleece, cloches or mini-tunnels – this protection will ensure that salads are not damaged and will continue to crop through to early spring. There's nothing worse than losing plants to an unexpected frost.

6

Plant autumn (overwintering) varieties of garlic such as 'Carcassonne Wight', as well as onion sets such as 'Shakespeare' and 'Red Winter'. Plant direct outside in a sunny spot and free-draining soil. You can also sow broad beans directly outside for an early harvest (this is especially useful if you don't have space to sow undercover in spring). All should begin to establish before the cold really sets in, surviving the winter as small plants, which will give them a head start the following spring.

Things to do

Late autumn

173

7

Succession sow microgreens into seed trays or shallow containers indoors. This will provide you with nutritious young seedlings and leaves for salads and garnishes. There are many autumn and winter mixes available containing mustards, oriental leaves and many other brassicas, all of which are quick to germinate and delicious.

8

Now is a good time to clean and oil any garden furniture or structures that may need preserving. When dry, rub away debris and algae growth using a stiff bush, then lightly sand before wiping down with a cloth. Finish off by applying a coat of Danish or linseed oil.

9

Prune rambling roses (see page 215) and blackberries by cutting out old growth, then tie in the long new growth so that is does not get damaged by any late autumn and winter storms. Large shrub roses and buddleia can also be pruned: reduce their size by about one third so that they don't suffer from wind rock and become loose in the soil.

10

Pots and containers of succulents and tender plants should be brought inside before they become damaged by the autumn rain and cold. Succulents and pelargoniums should be left to dry out and then watered infrequently so they remain relatively dry. This avoids them being sat wet and cold during winter, which could cause them to rot. Place them in a bright, cool spot (away from central heating) with good air circulation.

11

If living in a cold part of the UK, lift beetroots, carrots and potatoes before the winter frosts arrive. Remove the green tops if you've not already done so and then store the roots and tubers somewhere cool and dry until you are ready to use them. Packing them in a box of soil or sand and leaving them in a garage or shed is perfect.

12

As leaves fall, collect them from borders, paths, lawns and driveways. Gather the leaves together in a pile to begin the process of making next year's leaf mould. Use canes and some chicken wire to create a corral to scrape the leaves into and to prevent them from blowing way.

They will rot down over the year and provide you with a rich mulch. As with a compost heap, you can turn it periodically to speed up the process, though this is not essential.

Late autumn

Celebrate the season

Late autumn always seems to arrive with confidence, with its blustery winds and those odd bright days where the warmth from the sun feels extra special. There is an increased sense of space as the bare trees cast smaller shadows, making everywhere a little brighter and revealing bigger horizons. Dormice are curled up in their nests and reptiles and amphibians have tucked themselves away somewhere quiet for the winter. Just as in nature, it can be a time to hunker down and rest.

That said, walks and adventures are well rewarded at this time of year. In the dales and downs, mist can gather in the valleys, creating an eerie scene when viewed from a peak or summit. Scientifically known as cloud inversion (or temperature inversion), it occurs when cool air is trapped below a layer of warm air – this season's clear days and cool nights enable this to happen close to the ground. It's a truly magical moment to witness as the sun rises on a new day.

Harvest and forage

Swollen and glowing orange after a long hot summer, a pumpkin is the perfect tonic to any grey autumn days. Visually they seem to exude warmth, from their orange outer skin through to their peachy flesh. In truth, pumpkins are a form of winter squash and aren't always orange – they range in colour, shape and texture and have harder skins than their cousins, the summer squashes. While looking attractive on the harvest table, they also taste good. Traditionally they are used in spiced soups, roasted for curries or puréed in the American classic pumpkin pie, though more modern takes include salted pumpkin crème brûlée and pumpkin gnocchi.

I love to grow the classic-looking cucurbits 'Rouge Vif D'Etampes' and 'Musquee de Provence', along with the green, lumpy 'Marina di Chioggia', all of which have dense, creamy, aromatic and sweet flesh. On the squash side, delicious varieties include 'Uchiki Kuri' and 'Sweet Lightning', which, along with attractive ornamental gourds (pictured bottom left), will climb up and over structures. If you fancy growing something really fun, try 'Tromboncino' – a summer squash that will climb and form amazingly long fruits.

Though completely tender, squashes and pumpkins are easy to grow from seed: sow in late spring and they will be quick to germinate. Grow them on in pots and plant outside after the risk of frost has passed. They like lots of sun and a rich soil that's full of compost or well-rotted manure. Winter squashes and pumpkins should be cured, allowing the sun to dry and harden their skin, which will help with storage and flavour (see page 147).

Bat spotting

As the evenings draw in and darkness falls, the chances of seeing bats increases, albeit for a short time, as lowering temperatures will force them into a hibernation-like state for winter.

These nocturnal mammals dislike disturbance and light and so avoid human interaction where possible. The loss of safe roosting sites and disruption to their habitat has resulted in a dramatic crash in populations throughout the UK. Thankfully their plight has been recorded and now conservation efforts are helping to boost the numbers of some species.

As gardeners, we are in a position to help all wildlife by gardening in a way that promotes a biodiverse environment. Growing night-scented plants like *Nicotiana sylvestris* (tobacco plant) and *Oenothera stricta* 'Sulphurea' (evening primrose) encourages the night-flying insects bats feast on; including meadow and pond habitats helps even further.

While the best time to see bats ranges from April to November (when they are awake and breeding and rearing young), late autumn is when they are out and about, busy hunting to prepare for winter. They leave their roosts at dusk and you might see them around watercourses, edges of woodland, churchyards, parks and any other dark environments where nocturnal flying insects are about. Bats can be found in urban areas as well as forests, hedgerows and wetlands, always avoiding noisy, brightly lit places.

The common pipistrelle (*Pipistrellus pipistrellus*) is not fussy about where it roosts or what it feeds on, while the soprano pipistrelle (*Pipistrellus pygmaeus*) and Daubenton's bat (*Myotis daubentonii*) prefer to hunt over water.

Although their night vision is good, bats use echolocation to navigate and hunt, relying on sound to locate their prey. While you may hear the odd clicking or high-pitched noise, the majority of sound is beyond our hearing and specialist equipment is used to identify the different species. Look up your local bat conservation group which will be able to take you to sighting locations and teach you the best methods of spotting bats. In the UK, the Bat Conservation Trust is the place to start.

Have a bonfire celebration

There is something quite cathartic about having a bonfire at the end of the growing season, and not just for the practical reason of burning any garden waste that can't be reused, recycled or composted. The bonfire marks a poignant moment in the year, a coming together of loved ones around the flames as they hypnotically dance in the cool night air.

To ensure no wildlife is harmed and everyone remains safe, carefully plan where you are going to have your fire. Make sure it is sheltered from the wind and away from buildings, and that there is a generous clear space for the fire, as well as a source of cold water close by in case of accidents. If space is tight, a fire pit or outdoor stove is a good alternative to an open bonfire. Many also handily double up as barbecues or ovens.

Ideally fuel for the fire should be well seasoned, dry and cut to a manageable size. Dry leaves and cones are great for tinder, dry twigs and skinny branches for kindling, and bigger branches or untreated logs for fuel. I like to have a dedicated pile of fuel and build the fire from scratch to make sure there are no hedgehogs or other animals hiding in it – if you have made it in advance, always check for creatures before lighting. Burning leaves or fresh material should be done first as this is most likely to smoke or spit.

As the fire burns, hot embers with little flames will form at the base – these are to be encouraged by adding more wooden material and then waiting, creating the perfect fire to cook on. Toasting sweet chestnuts is a traditional option, although buttered sweetcorn, stewed apple or damper bread on skewers are all good.

For something a little fancier, try making foil parcels that can be placed directly on the hot embers or on to a baking plate or grill. Sliced or jacket potatoes work well, while fish is also a good option; salmon with lemon and tarragon is a personal favourite. And I think it's essential to finish with toasted marshmallows.

Late autumn

Winter

Early winter

As daylight hours ebb away and we move towards the shortest day of the year, the drop in temperatures announces the arrival of winter. Outside it feels as though the garden and countryside are taking a well-earned rest. Of the deciduous trees, all but the stubborn oaks and trimmed beeches have lost their leaves and are offering a tracery of twigs and branches that decorate views.

It's the time of year when I get a rare feeling that I could happily skip to later in season, but then I remind myself there is still much to be getting on with. Contrary to the common perception that winter is a quiet time for the gardener, there's a lot to do and think about; tidying beds and borders, clearing and cutting back previous seasons' growth and mulching beds in preparation for the early spring bulbs to appear are just a few of the tasks to keep busy with.

As comfortingly predictable as tradition, stocks of bare-root roses, trees, shrubs and fruit become available, making this a great time to get planting, though be mindful that anything slightly tender has to wait until early spring. Much pruning and training occurs now and continues throughout the winter, from apples and pears to roses and soft fruit; with a snip and a tuck, trees are brought back to a neat frame, while climbing roses are gently strapped to their supports.

Despite the long list of jobs, there's always enough time to stop and fall in tune with the slower pace that the natural world has adopted. Be sure to enjoy these quiet moments, as in no time at all, the excitement and growth of spring will return.

Plants in season

The cold weather can be a full stop to the growing year, as many plants stand still. However, there are still some that are preparing to flower or come into growth. Witch hazels bud up and *Garrya elliptica* (silk tassel bush) elongates its catkins, while *Cyclamen coum* (eastern cyclamen) and *Helleborus niger* (Christmas rose) begin to flower, with early primulas in tow. Early winter has more to offer than flowers, though – stems, berries and seedheads also become prominent, especially when set against the solid backdrop of an evergreen shrub or hedge.

Acer griseum →
PAPERBARK MAPLE

A slow-growing, ornamental tree with attractive cinnamon-like peeling bark. Acid-green flowers appear with the young leaves in spring, giving a soft appearance and casting little shade. Come autumn, the foliage turns fiery shades before falling and allowing the bark to take centre stage. Gradually forming a broad canopy, this deciduous tree is perfect for smaller spaces. It prefers full sun or light shade, away from drying winds, and it can be planted in any soil that is not waterlogged in winter. Purchase and plant trees from late autumn to early spring. *Hardy throughout most of the UK (RHS H5, USDA 7b/8a). H x S: 8 x 6m.*

Calamagrostis × acutiflora 'Karl Foerster'

FEATHER REED-GRASS 'KARL FOERSTER'

A reliable perennial grass with architectural seedheads that stand appealingly through winter. Soft mounds of fine, dark green foliage erupt from the ground in spring to form tussocks that support flower stems holding iridescent plumes during summer. In autumn the flowers tighten, changing to buff-coloured vertical spears and creating visual drama that persists through winter. Great in naturalistic schemes or for winter interest in borders. Best in full sun in well-drained soil. Buy plants or make divisions in early spring. *Hardy throughout most of the UK (RHS H6, USDA 6b/7a). H x S: 1.5m x 50cm.*

Chasmanthium latifolium

NORTH AMERICAN WILD OATS

A deciduous ornamental grass that makes a show at this time of year with dried foliage and interesting flattened seedheads. Cut back in early spring for new foliage in late spring with broad fresh green blades. It continues to grow through summer forming an upright, well-behaved clump with decorative, oat-like flower heads appearing in early autumn. These dry to a fawn colour, dangling on wiry stems that remain attractive through the winter. Plant in full sun or part shade in free-draining, moisture-retentive soil. Sow seeds or buy container-grown plants in spring. *Hardy throughout most of the UK (RHS H6, USDA 6b/7a). H x S: 1m x 50cm.*

Cornus sanguinea 'Midwinter Fire' ↑

DOGWOOD 'MIDWINTER FIRE'

An uplifting deciduous shrub with stems glowing bright during winter; the tips burn an orange red that gradually transitions to a mellow yellow lower down. During spring and summer oval leaves hide the colourful stems and white flowers, before turning yellow and falling in autumn. The younger stems hold the best colour, so some judicious pruning is required. Lovely planted near water where the colour can be reflected. Happiest in full sun, though will take light shade and any reasonable soil. Purchase and plant container-grown shrubs in spring or autumn, or take hardwood cuttings in autumn. *Hardy throughout most of the UK (RHS H6, USDA 6b/7a). H x S: 2 x 2m.*

Early winter

Dipsacus fullonum →
WILD TEASEL

An ornamental biennial wildflower that has architectural beauty throughout the season. Rumpled, thistle-like leaves form a flat rosette during the first year from which tall, spiked, upright stems arise the following spring. Ornamental cones top the stems, holding tiny, pale lilac flowers that are adored by butterflies and bees. As the season goes on the stems and flowers dry for winter decoration, holding seeds treasured by finches. A fantastic native for a gravel garden, meadow or naturalistic border edge. Best in a sunny to lightly shaded location in most soils. Sow seeds direct or in modules in autumn or spring. *Fully hardy throughout the UK (RHS H7, USDA 6a-1). H x S: 2m x 50cm.*

Phlomis russeliana
TURKISH SAGE

A tough herbaceous perennial with large, soft, grey-green leaves that are semi-evergreen and provide a ruffled carpet, from which the stout flower stems arise in summer, carrying whorls of primrose-yellow flowers. By autumn the flowers have gone, leaving the dried calyces that held them to decorate the stems as they stand through winter into spring. Perfect for the front of a mixed border, or gravel or Mediterranean garden. Plant container-grown plants during the growing season; alternatively, sow seed or divide in early spring. *Hardy throughout most of the UK (RHS H6, USDA 6b/7a). H x S: 80cm x 1m.*

Pinus strobus 'Torulosa' →
TWISTED WHITE PINE

A medium-sized evergreen tree that grows from a compact shaggy dome to an upright pyramidal canopy that's densely covered in attractive blue-green needles. Mature specimens have the addition of attractive pointed cones that persist through winter and into the following year. Reasonably slow growing and architectural in form, this pine is perfect as a low-maintenance feature in a sunny lawn or border. Grows best in full sun in a rich but free-draining soil. Container-grown plants can be purchased throughout the year. It is best planted in autumn or spring. *Fully hardy throughout the UK (RHS H7, USDA 6a-1). H x S: 7 x 2m.*

Pittosporum tenuifolium 'Silver Sheen' ↑
TAWHIWHI 'SILVER SHEEN'

Attractive, tiny, silvery evergreen leaves decorate the thin stems of this multi-branched shrub, giving it a fine, graceful appearance. During early summer, discrete burgundy flowers appear on the stems offering a light, sweet scent. While happy to be left naturally soft in habit, it can be clipped into a hedge or topiary to introduce an evergreen structural element to the garden. Enjoys full sun to light shade in any free-draining soil and in a position sheltered from cold winds. Buy and plant container-grown specimens in spring or late summer; take semi-ripe cuttings in late summer. *Hardy throughout most of the UK (RHS H4, USDA 8b/9a). H x S: 5 x 3m.*

Rosa × odorata 'Mutabilis' ↑
ROSE 'MUTABILIS'

A floriferous tea rose for late-season interest with tutti-frutti-coloured flowers that continue right up to the first frosts. It has an open habit and lax, thornless stems that hold burgundy young foliage. The flowers are pink in bud opening to a buff apricot before aging to pink, which give it an elegant yet slightly tropical appearance. It repeat flowers from summer through to the beginning of winter when the flowers are accompanied by numerous small, green hips. Great for the mixed border or within naturalistic plantings. Plant in full sun in rich, fertile but free-draining soil. Purchase and plant bare-root stock in winter. *Hardy throughout most of the UK (RHS H5, USDA 7b/8a). H x S: 1.5 x 1.5m.*

Skimmia japonica
JAPANESE SKIMMIA

A low-growing, branched, evergreen shrub with bottle green leaves that form a tidy dome. Flowering in spring, male plants have larger, more conspicuous and fragrant flowers than female plants, though the demure female flowers develop shiny, bright red berries that hold on right through winter and into spring. Ideal for shady borders and around buildings. A woodland-dwelling shrub, it prefers a shady to part-shaded spot in rich, moist but free-draining soil with a slightly acidic pH. Purchase plants or take soft-tip cuttings in spring, or semi-ripe cuttings in late summer. *Hardy throughout most of the UK (RHS H5, USDA 7b/8a). H x S: 1.3 x 1.3m.*

Rubus cockburnianus ↑
WHITE-STEMMED BRAMBLE

A deciduous shrub that for much of the growing season looks like any other bramble, with small purple flowers in early summer followed by unpalatable fruits. Come autumn the foliage falls to reveal glowing white stems that shine brightly on the dullest of days. It eventually forms a thicket, so prune out the oldest stems at the base to encourage new growth with the best colouring. A striking focal point in a shrub border or wild garden. Plant in any soil in full sun. Plant container-grown stock in spring or summer, or take semi-ripe cuttings in late summer or hardwood cuttings in winter. *Hardy throughout most of the UK (RHS H6, USDA 6b/7a). H x S: 3 x 3.5m.*

Veronicastrum virginicum 'Erica'
CULVER'S ROOT 'ERICA'

A tall, upright and elegant herbaceous perennial with attractive flowers in summer and interesting seedheads through winter. Emerging in spring, the stems hold whorls of foliage that by late summer are tipped with elongated, dark pink spires that transition to pale pink as the flowers open. By winter they have dried to a rusty brown and will stand through most of the season. A perfect border plant, working well in cultivated and naturalistic settings. Plant in full sun to light shade in any reasonable soil that is free-draining in winter. Purchase and plant in spring, or divide in early spring. *Fully hardy throughout the UK (RHS H7, USDA 6a–1). H x S: 1.5m x 50cm.*

Early winter

Things to do

Plant a tree

While so many things in this world are fast paced and transient, a tree is a symbol of stability. The environmental benefits of planting trees is immeasurable: they help to provide the oxygen that we breathe, support complex webs of life, create shade and prevent soil erosion. As a gardener, one of the greatest legacies you can leave is a tree ... or twenty!

1 Trees are an investment of money and time, so think carefully before you make any decisions: size, ornamental value and ecological benefits should help you decide. Consider whether to buy a container-grown tree (available all year) or bare-root (available in winter). Bare-root stock can be cheaper and the root systems are never pot bound. Young trees will establish faster than mature ones, requiring less staking and future watering.

2 Getting the planting hole right is the first step to success. Planting a tree too deep can affect its health and growth. Look for the root flare at the base of the trunk (where the trunk naturally widens and joins the roots) – this should sit just above the soil level. Dig the planting hole and keep checking the depth using a straight stick to bridge the hole and simulate the depth. The roots should fit in the hole with about a 10cm gap all around.

3 The base of the hole doesn't require digging over, place the tree into position, making sure it is vertical and has the best side facing forward. Back fill, checking the tree's position and firming the soil as you go. You do not need to add any manure or compost, but you can add mycorrhizal fungi, which will help the tree establish. Firm the soil using your feet – it doesn't matter if it is slightly mounded as it will settle, just remember the root flare should be above the soil level.

4 To prevent weed growth and to feed the tree, mulch (6–8cm deep) around the tree, avoiding contact with the trunk/root flare. You may need to stake the tree so that it has support while new roots begin to anchor it. Angle the post to point into the prevailing wind so that it crosses the trunk at no higher than half the overall height of the tree. Larger trees can be root anchored by fixing them underground with wires. Guards may also be needed to prevent damage from rabbits and deer.

5 Water thoroughly to settle the tree in. You may also need to prune it to encourage it to branch and develop a balanced canopy.

Plant a hedge

From a human perspective, hedges are a great way of dividing spaces or marking boundaries and to formally or informally provide structure and seasonal interest. From an ecological perspective, they can simulate a woodland edge and can be a biologically rich space that's home to many different species. If you're looking to define an area in your garden, create some privacy or hide something unsightly, think about using a hedge rather than a man-made structure for the additional benefits that it will bring.

1 When deciding on your hedge, size and style will come into play. Traditional choices for large, smart hedges include *Taxus* (yew), *Fagus* (beech), *Carpinus* (hornbeam) and *Prunus lusitanica* (Portuguese laurel), as well as the conifer options, including *Thuja plicata* (western red cedar) and *Chamaecyparis lawsoniana* (Lawson's cyprus). A mixed native hedge will give a more informal look and provide a diverse range of plants for wildlife. It could include *Cornus sanguinea* (common dogwood), *Crataegus monogyna* (common hawthorn), *Euonymus europaeus* (spindle), *Ilex aquifolium* (common holly), *Prunus spinosa* (blackthorn) and *Rosa canina* (dog rose). For smaller hedges try dwarf cultivars of *Berberis thunbergii* (Japanese barberry), *Lonicera pileata* (box-leaved honeysuckle) and *Pittosporum tenuifolium* (tawhiwhi), along with *Hebe pinguifolia* 'Sutherlandii'. Clipped herbs such as lavender and rosemary can look pleasing, or alternatively try a soft edging like *Teucrium × lucidrys* (hybrid germander). Due to problems with box moth caterpillar and box blight, traditional box should be avoided.

2 Mark out where your hedge will be and measure the length to work out the number of plants to order. Spacing varies depending on plant size and species, but the supplier's website will specify the details. A general guide is to space plants about 40–50cm apart. Planting closer will give you a more instant effect, but also produce a slower-growing hedge as plants compete for resources (which can actually be ideal if you'd like to restrict the size of the hedge).

3 Prepare the intended hedge line for planting: this could involve removing turf or clearing weeds. A width of approximately 50cm should be ample for a single line of hedging, although you will have to go wider if you are planting a double or staggered (zigzag) row of plants.

4 Before planting, check the plants over and remove any snapped stems or

bare roots that have been damaged during transit. Then position the plants along your prepared site to ensure even spacing. Plant sizes may differ so mix the smaller and bigger plants evenly along the row. To plant, begin at one end and dig a hole, place the plant in and backfill, checking the plants are straight before you firm the soil down. You may wish to apply mycorrhizal fungi around the roots first, to help aid establishment. Remember not to plant too deep (follow the advice planting a tree on page 190). Once planted, water in well.

5   Mulch the plants using a compost or organic matter to feed the soil, limit competition from weeds and promote healthy establishment of the hedge. If your young hedge is on an exposed, windy site install a temporary windbreak fence (available online or from garden centres), which will protect it and enable quicker establishment. Large hedging plants (1.2m or taller) may need staking: create a low rail using upright posts and long lengths of timber.

Prepare for next year

With cold rainy days a regular occurrence in winter, embracing the outside may not always be so appealing. Besides, working on sodden ground doesn't make for good gardening practice. On these indoor days you can use your time wisely at home, or perhaps in the shed or greenhouse, to get organised for next year's growing season and to help things run a little bit smoother.

Now is a good time to get all machinery serviced so it is clean, in working order and ready to use before you store it away for the winter. Cutting tools that remain by your side through these darker months can also be sharpened, cleaned and lubricated, making them a pleasure to use.

Consult any notes you've made through the year and use this time to research solutions to problems that you encountered or new projects that you are hoping to embark on. This could be anything from biological pest control through to specific plant varieties you want to try, pruning techniques to learn or composting methods to employ. Take a critical look at your planting: celebrate what has worked well and make a plan for areas that you feel need improving.

Order and source tools and materials. Buying in bulk with friends is a good way to lower costs on items and reduce delivery costs for things like peat-free compost. Try to think of the environment and use sustainable materials where possible, for example, hazel rods or bean poles are great for all manner of garden tasks when coupled with jute string. Look around the house to see what throwaway objects you can save and reuse: loo rolls are perfect for sowing sweet peas and cut-down milk cartons make cheap seed trays.

Schedule your tasks ahead of time. Jobs such as repairing a trellis or painting gates will require better weather and some planning. Other jobs, such as cleaning slippery surfaces or topping up gravel paths can be completed on a damp day. The important thing is to be organised, listing the jobs so that you can make the most of any weather.

Take stock of any seeds that you already have, checking varieties and viability with 'best before' dates. Plan and list all of the other plants you wish to grow from seed and that you need to order so that you have all of them ready before spring begins. I like to list which seeds I should sow in what season (see page 18), and group seeds into piles depending on when they should be sown. This will save you time during the busy spring period and will hopefully prevent you from forgetting any.

Early winter

Task list

Jobs to do during early winter

1

Harvest the last of the seed that you wish to collect for this year. Leave it somewhere to dry (empty vegetable trays on a windowsill are perfect) before cleaning it. Pack in labelled envelopes (with a name and date) and then store in a tin somewhere dry and cool (see page 114).

2

Insulate any garden taps or turn off water supplies to the garden. Unprotected, these may become frozen during the late winter months and cause damage to pipes that will result in leaks.

3

Check and clear gutters, downpipes, gullies and any drainage channels so water can run freely. This should help avoid any damage from potential flooding during winter. If not already installed, add a water butt to save water and reduce reliance on the hosepipe during summer.

4

Begin planting bare-root roses. Inspect the plant on arrival and prune stems back to a strong node (the small bump where a bud emerges) and trim any roots that are excessively long or damaged. Dig a hole that's wide enough to accommodate the roots and at a depth that ensures the graft union (the swollen area at the base) will sit above the soil level. Place the rose in the hole and back fill, firming with your hand or foot. Water and mulch around the base to aid establishment.

5

Create a bean or celeriac trench. Dig a channel where you plan to grow these crops next year and make it approximately 40cm deep and 40cm wide, and extend it to your preferred length. Over winter, fill the trench with any vegetable scraps from the kitchen. When the trench is full, cover them up with the soil as early spring arrives. The rotting plant material will make sure your hungry crops get off to a great start in spring.

6

Cold mornings are a good time to turn your compost and incorporate oxygen that will help with the decomposition process. If you only have one bin, empty the contents on to a sheet or piece of flat cardboard before refilling your bin with the material you just emptied. If any is ready, then use as a mulch or soil improver. If you have a series of bins, you can empty any compost that is ready and then shift the contents of the other bins along.

Things to do

197

7

Clean paths, decks and terraces that have become slippery with algae and moss during the wet weather. A stiff brush or pressure washer will work on most surfaces. Gravel and aggregate paths should be weeded and raked, as well as topped up with more aggregate if needed to give the garden a fresh look.

8

As light levels and day length decrease, it's time to remove shading from greenhouses. Blinds and screens can be stored, while shading paint can be washed off. It's a good idea to wash all the outside glazing where dirt and algae may have settled, as this will help to improve light penetration and support plants as they cope with the short, dark days.

9

Check on fruit and vegetables that have been harvested and are in storage. Anything that is damaged should be used first before it begins to rot and any rotting fruit or vegetables should be removed. Check for rodent damage, too – creatures find this stored food just as appetising as we do.

10

Protect terracotta pots from frost damage by lifting them off the ground. This allows water to drain freely while preventing freezing ground temperatures from permeating up into the pot. You can also use fleece or hessian/burlap to wrap around the outside of the pot, protecting it from cold air temperatures and sudden thawing in the morning sun (pictured on page 197).

11

If you're leaving dahlias in the ground over winter, mulch heavily to protect tubers from the cold. If lifting them, wait until the stems have been blackened by frost before cutting them down to near the ground. Gently dig up the tubers and leave them to dry somewhere cool and frost-free before cleaning off the worst of the soil. Store for winter in a cardboard box or crate somewhere frost-free.

12

Continue to harvest the last of the aubergines, chillies and tomatoes from the greenhouse. Salad leaves and herbs should be cropping if given protection, while pea shoots will be growing slowly, in time for a late winter and early spring harvest. Outside, beetroots, carrots, celeriac, fennel, kale, leeks, parsnips, potatoes and Brussels sprouts should all be available to harvest.

Early winter

Celebrate the season

Like a fading ember, any remaining autumn warmth dwindles as we approach the winter solstice. This is the shortest day of the year and marks the moment when Earth is at its maximum tilt away from the sun. There is much celebration associated with this time, from the Pagan Yule, which honours fire and the warmth it brings, to Judaism's Hanukkah and Shab-e Chelleh in Iran, which marks the victory of light over darkness as the solstice passes.

Outside, fieldfares and waxwings arrive to take advantage of the last autumnal fruit and winter berries, while foxes and tawny owls search for a mate, ensuring the arrival of their young coincides with the richness of spring. I find it remarkable that even in the darkest days of winter, nature finds opportunities and looks forward to the seasons ahead.

Harvest and forage

After a summer of leafy growth and an autumn of expanding, the mighty celeriac is ready to harvest in early winter. It's a long-season vegetable that requires a little effort, but is worth the trouble as it can stand hardy through winter and last well into the new year. Sow seed undercover in early spring into trays and then prick out into modules. The little plants should be grown on indoors and planted out after the risk of frost has passed. Celeriac prefers a sunny spot in moist, rich, free-draining soil, and it's good to add additional compost to the planting area. Remember that celeriac loves moisture, so water through any dry periods. By late summer you should be stripping the outer lower leaves from the base and can continue to do so into autumn. Through autumn the roots swell dramatically creating the familiar globe shape, that indicates they are ready for harvesting. 'Monarch' and 'Prinz' are both reliable varieties and produce a crop that will add something special to winter meals; their nutty, spiced flavour can enhance stews or be simply enjoyed roasted (my favourite).

If celeriac is a little something extra, then leek is the essential winter vegetable. Sow seed into a deep tray or patch of soil in spring; the former allows you to germinate them indoors a little earlier. Let the young leeks grow until almost pencil size (hence the deep tray), at which point (usually early summer) they should be carefully lifted and replanted deeply. Lightly trim the tips of the leaves and roots to make the leeks easier to handle. Space them about 15cm apart and leave 15cm between rows. A good autumn variety is 'Stamford', while 'Blauwgroene Winter'-Bandit and 'Musselburgh' will be ready in winter. 'Northern Lights' has purple tints to its blue foliage, while 'Zermatt' can be cropped in late summer as 'baby' leeks.

Force bulbs

For many of us, the grey, wet weather and long dark nights can be a little oppressive. While having seasonal berries, twigs and greenery in the house can be uplifting, there is nothing that can compete with the sweet smell and colour of hyacinths or paperwhite narcissi. With a little preparation, you can enjoy these beauties though the darkest months.

Forcing bulbs describes bringing them into growth early, forcing them with a period of cold and then warmth to trick them into believing spring has arrived. While many naturally early varieties like *Narcissus* 'Avalanche' and 'Erlicheer' can be used, amaryllis, hyacinths and paperwhite narcissi are the most traditional. You can buy bulbs in autumn with your other spring bulbs – just make sure they are 'prepared', meaning they have had a period of cold.

The ideal container is one that is sturdy and heavy, so that it won't topple over when the bulbs have reached full height. For amaryllis, I would use a deep pot and saucer; for hyacinths and narcissi, go for something shallow and wide like a ceramic bowl, so that you can fit in several bulbs. Ensure the pot has drainage holes.

I have the luxury of a greenhouse, so I start my bulbs off in individual pots in a free-draining, peat-free compost, and then plant them into their final container when they are actively growing. If space is at a premium, you can plant them into their final containers straight away. To do this, place the bulbs close to the surface of the peat-free compost to give them as much space for root growth as possible. They do not have to be as deep as they would be in the ground, and the neck and shoulders of the bulb can be showing. You can decorate the container with moss and twigs to provide interest while the bulbs are growing, and the latter also offer support when the plants are taller.

Different varieties require different growing periods before flowering, so check individual recommendations if timing is important – if you want them for Christmas, you may need to plant your bulbs in early autumn. Personally, I prefer them in flower for the new year, when things can feel a little flat, so I plant some bulbs every two weeks or so throughout autumn and early winter for a succession of flowers. Once planted, water and grow on a warm and bright windowsill. When the flower buds form, move to somewhere a little cooler to prolong the flowering time.

After flowering, remove the flowering stem and continue to grow on. Hyacinths can be planted out in the garden, but will need hardening off, while amaryllis and paperwhites are tender and should be protected from the frost.

Celebrate the season

203

Make natural decorations

With the festive season approaching it is time to start thinking about decorating the home. I love to use all manner of foliage, twigs and seedheads collected from the garden or foraged on walks. Combined with a little imagination and preparation, you can create magical decorations that celebrate nature at Christmas and into the new year.

The first rule to remember is that there are no rules ... it's always worth trying something to see if it works. That said, some preparation is key and I like to collect seedheads and flowers throughout the year, hanging them to dry while they are in good condition (see page 103). This is particularly important for showstoppers such as alliums and hydrangeas – the former look great hanging with teasels, while hydrangea heads look beautiful in garlands. Other materials such as cones and lichen-covered twigs can also be gathered in advance.

For foliage, evergreens with glossy leaves are ideal as they tend to last several days without water. I use a mix of ivy, bay and rosemary to create a medley of leaf shape and texture. The contrasting foliage of holly, eucalyptus, osmanthus and pittosporum add further interest. Coloured stems of dogwood and willow can look good, as can magnolia branches with large furry buds and larch twigs, which often carry small cones.

Seedheads such as teasels and eryngiums work really well, their skeletal frames already look wintery. *Allium* 'Purple Sensation' or 'Cristophii' are excellent, along with the starburst-like *A. schubertii*. From the border I like to take spires of dried veronicastrum and soft heads of chasmanthium and miscanthus, as well as cardoon and giant fennel seedheads. You may wish to spray these with a touch of gold, bronze or snow, though go steady as less is definitely more.

Last to cut are the berries, hips and fruits. I treat these like cut flowers, resting them in water for a day or two after cutting and before using. Holly berries are the classic option, but I find the pigeons have usually eaten them, so I prefer to use skimmia berries. Rosehips are a pretty addition and can be found on most roses. Large ramblers such as *Rosa filipes* 'Kiftsgate' and *R.* 'Seagull' have sprays of small delicate hips, while *R. moyesii* and *R.* 'Herbstfeuer' have larger, eye-catching displays.

Whether I'm making a wreath, table centrepiece or garland, I tend to make a base with the foliage first. This can be arranged in vases, although it will last a week or so out of water and arranged in situ. Once the base is constructed, I add lights or candle holders before embellishing with the final details of seedheads, cones, berries and twigs.

Late winter

If winter feels like it is lingering, take comfort from the fact that the short days are gradually getting longer, even if it is at a glacial pace. Every so often, a sunny day arrives and that's always a wonderful reminder to make the most of this time and its pleasures.

These bright days bring excitement to the garden and the countryside beyond; the low sun casts long, dramatic shadows and creates striking visual effects. It's a time to celebrate the 'bones' of the garden, the permanent structure provided by woody trees and shrubs, hedges and hard landscaping. Clear conditions at night often deliver freezing temperatures, allowing nature to paint these white with frost, transforming the garden into something magical come morning. It's a really peaceful and beautiful time to be outside. The cold air can leave your face and lungs feeling refreshed, while sparkling icy crystals cling to surfaces, highlighting details that usually go unnoticed.

Although the garden gently sleeps, there are things to be getting on with. Gardening really is about sowing seeds, in both the physical and metaphorical sense. What you do now in (and for) your garden will have a dramatic effect on how it looks and behaves during spring and summer. That said, it's too early to begin sowing actual seeds, though exceptions include starting early sweet peas, microgreens and pea shoots indoors.

At times, when the wintry weather gets a bit unbearable, retreating inside to research and organise what you plan to sow and grow later in the year will prove invaluable to your future gardening success and your enjoyment.

Plants in season

The wet, cold and sometimes freezing weather banishes any soft and lush plant growth from the garden in the latter half of winter. For the majority, new flowers and leaves remain tucked away in tight buds until conditions improve, and all but the toughest seedheads will have begun to deteriorate, so the garden can feel a little lacklustre. Despite this there are still many interesting plants, some with vibrant stem colour, textural bark, coloured foliage or even flowers. These plants become horticultural heroes, with their botanical offerings cherished by many a gardener in a period when new life is scarce.

Bergenia 'Eric Smith' →
ELEPHANT'S EARS 'ERIC SMITH'

A rhizomatous, evergreen perennial that has large, round, thick leaves throughout the year, giving the plant its common name. During winter they change from a polished mid-green to deep maroon, appearing almost metallic with burnished bronze tints. In spring, glowing pink flowers hang like bells from fleshy stems just above the new green foliage. While lovely in spring, the winter appeal makes it perfect for the front of a border, or alongside a path or terrace. Bergenia can grow happily in full sun to light shade in most reasonable soils. Plant divisions or container-grown plants in spring or autumn. *Fully hardy throughout the UK (RHS H7, USDA 6a-1). H x S: 40 x 80cm.*

Cyclamen coum →
EASTERN CYCLAMEN

A mighty tuberous perennial in every sense except stature. Dormant below the soil for the summer and autumn months, its small round leaves begin to appear in winter, carpeting the ground with dark green and silver foliage. From late winter, flowers appear above the ornate foliage, ranging from brilliant white to gleaming pink. These tough plants will take the frost and snow and still continue to flower, lifting one's spirit on a dull day. Prefers part shade and a free-draining soil. Works well planted under and around deciduous trees and shrubs or in containers, and will naturalise if left undisturbed. Plant container-grown plants in early spring. *Hardy throughout most of the UK (RHS H5, USDA 7b/8a). H x S: 10 x 10cm.*

Cynara cardunculus →
CARDOON

A majestic perennial with ragged, silvery leaves that appear in winter and offer attractive texture and form. As the growing season begins, the leaves grow in size and quantity as they erupt from the ground. The show culminates in early summer with tall flower stems (up to 3m in height!) crowned with impressive thistle-like flowers. Cardoons make a striking focal point within a herbaceous border, kitchen or gravel garden if given adequate space. Best in full sun and in a free-draining soil. Plant container-grown plants in spring. *Hardy throughout most of the UK (RHS H5, USDA 7b/8a). H x S: 3 x 1.5m.*

Late winter

Daphne bholua 'Jacqueline Postill' ↑
DAPHNE 'JACQUELINE POSTILL'

An understated, semi-evergreen shrub with an upright and well-behaved habit. For much of the year it has narrow, oval-shaped leaves with a dark green sheen. From late winter to early spring, terminal clusters of pinkish-white, tubular flowers open to release a sweet fragrance that generously fills the air – an absolute joy for this time of year! Requires very little pruning and is perfect for a woodland garden or shrubbery. Best in a sheltered spot in full sun to light shade, and in any rich soil that does not sit wet in winter. Plant container-grown plants in spring or autumn. *Hardy throughout most of the UK, except the coldest pockets (RHS H4, USDA 8b/9a). H x S: 2.5 x 1m.*

Ferula communis ↑
GIANT FENNEL

A goliath-sized, short-lived herbaceous perennial that produces large globes of acid-yellow flowers during spring, held high on tall, thick stems. Along with this dramatic display, the fennel offers the benefit of coming into growth in winter, decorating borders with fluffy mounds of finely cut foliage in the most welcome green. Perfect for a herb potager, gravel garden or naturalistic plantings. Best grown in full sun and on any reasonable soil that drains freely in winter. Sow fresh seed trays in autumn and leave outside to germinate, or plant container-grown plants in spring. *Hardy throughout most of the UK, except the coldest pockets (RHS H4, USDA 8b/9a). H x S: 3 x 1m.*

← *Galanthus nivalis*
COMMON SNOWDROP

A bulbous perennial that has a simple charm but can form impressive swaths that take your breath away! In late winter, strappy leaves appear, followed by softly fragrant flowers which hang in an elegant droop. The foliage continues into spring, feeding the bulbs for next year's display, before dying back in summer. Perfect for brightening up the last of the winter days, it will bulk up to form clumps that can be lifted, split and replanted after flowering. Grow under deciduous trees or among perennials where dormant bulbs will enjoy summer shade. Grow in any reasonable, moist and free-draining soil. Plant 'in the green' either from container-grown stock or bare-root plants in early spring. *Hardy throughout most of the UK (RHS H5, USDA 7b/8a). H x S: 10 x 10cm.*

← *Hamamelis* × *intermedia* 'Aphrodite'
WITCH HAZEL 'APHRODITE'

A choice, deciduous woodland shrub with a spreading habit and wavy-edged leaves that turn golden before falling in autumn. The naked stems hold clusters of flower buds that open in late winter. 'Aphrodite' has yellow-orange petals that unfurl from burgundy calyces. Although the flowers are individually small, en masse they are spectacular and sweetly scented. A well-behaved plant, it requires minimal pruning and prefers sun or part shade in most soils that are not alkaline or waterlogged. Plant grafted plants in autumn or spring. *Hardy throughout most of the UK (RHS H5, USDA 7b/8a). H x S: 3 x 3m.*

Late winter

Helleborus × *hybridus* →

A reliable and versatile herbaceous
perennial known for its floriferous display.
The valuable cupped flowers come in a
variety of colours and bashfully hang to
conceal their various markings and petal
arrangement from casual onlookers. The
flowers last well into spring, when they
are superseded by large, leathery, palmate
leaves that form loose mounds during
the growing season. The semi-evergreen
leaves can look tatty in late winter, so cut
and remove them before the flowering
stems emerge. Perfect for woodland
gardens and shady borders, it prefers light
sun to part shade in any reasonable soil.
Plant container-grown plants in spring
when plants are still flowering. *Fully hardy
throughout the UK (RHS H7, USDA 6a-1).
H x S: 40 x 40cm.*

Primula 'Barnhaven Blue' →
PRIMULA 'BARNHAVEN BLUE'

A dependable, semi-evergreen perennial
with vigour. It quickly bulks up to form
strong clumps of foliage and flowers, and
throughout the year rosettes of rumpled
leaves quietly grow below taller plants.
During late winter, central clusters of
buds begin to open, presenting flowers in
shades of blue, from the palest cornfield
to deep savoy. Good for underplanting
trees and shrubs and mixing with
perennials. Best in light sun to part shade
in any reasonable soil. Plant container-
grown plants or divisions in spring or
autumn. *Hardy throughout most of the UK
(RHS H6, USDA 6b/7a). H x S: 15 x 20cm.*

Salix gracilistyla 'Mount Aso'

A bushy deciduous shrub that lacks the extreme vigour of other willows. During the growing season the multi-branched stems carry simple bluish-green leaves. In late winter, when the leaves have fallen, the routine look is discarded and stems become decorated with pink buds. Each bud is covered in tiny hairs, giving it a silvery sheen and fluffy pink appearance right into spring when the upright catkins emerge. Grow where the winter spectacle can be appreciated. Best in full sun in moist but well-drained soil. Plant container-grown plants in spring or autumn; take hardwood cuttings in late winter. *Hardy throughout most of the UK (RHS H5, USDA 7b/8a). H x S: 3.5 x 3.5m.*

Rhododendron 'Wine and Roses' ↑

RHODODENDRON 'WINE AND ROSES'

A slow-growing, dwarf rhododendron that packs a punch in both flower and evergreen foliage. Throughout the year, this compact plant has sultry dark green leaves with contrasting burgundy undersides. In late spring, buds burst open to reveal the attractive pink flowers with petal edges beautifully stained with blackcurrant. Perfect for the front of a shrubbery, small border or even large container, offering evergreen structure. Best in light sun to dappled shade in an acidic loam soil. Plant container-grown plants in autumn to allow them to establish before they flower in spring. *Hardy throughout most of the UK (RHS H5, USDA 7b/8a). H x S: 1 x 1m.*

Sarcococca confusa

SWEET BOX

A restrained evergreen shrub with compact growth and masses of small, glossy leaves that are the perfect filler for the back of a border. Sitting quietly throughout the year, sarcococca comes alive in late winter. Inconspicuous though highly fragrant ivory-white flowers appear tight to the stem, filling the air with their sweet scent. Black or purple berries follow and persist into the following winter before dropping in the hope of establishing new plants. Unfussy, sarcococca will grow in any reasonable soil in dappled sun to full shade. Plant container-grown plants in spring or autumn. *Hardy throughout most of the UK (RHS H5, USDA 7b/8a). H x S: 1.5 x 1.5m.*

Late winter

Things to do

Prune roses

As with many trees and shrubs, roses require pruning to promote health and vigour, and to encourage an abundance of flowers and a pleasing shape. Different rose types call for different pruning methods, which can get a little confusing, but if you can identify the type of rose you have, and if you follow the main principles of pruning (see page 13), you shouldn't go wrong.

Do note that some roses will require support and training at this time of year. Climbers and ramblers work best against a building, wall, fence or large tree, while shrub roses with soft, lax growth can be trained over a free-standing support. When tying in stems, it is best to use a natural jute twine, which will eventually rot and won't cut into the stems.

BUSH Roses are tough plants and many respond well to a hard prune in winter, particularly bush forms like hybrid teas and floribundas. Cut back the previous season's growth to a semi-permanent framework, but leave a section of the new stem that's about 8cm in length and has three or four healthy buds. Lateral shoots can also be trimmed a little shorter (about 5cm in length). On established plants it may be necessary to remove one or two of the main stems, cutting as low to the ground as possible to relieve congestion.

SHRUB These include many of the species roses and old garden roses, such as alba, damask and centifolia. Many will produce a single flush of flowers and can be pruned in late summer after they have flowered (if you don't want winter hips). Shrub roses require a lighter touch than bush types as their growth is usually less vigorous. Remove up to one third of the current season's growth and cut the lateral stems to three or four leaves/buds.

REPEAT FLOWERING SHRUB These include bourbon, china and portland types and should be pruned in winter, although light deadheading in summer will encourage repeat flowering. Again, remove up to one third of the current season's growth and shorten laterals. On established plants, remove one or two of the main stems cutting them close to the ground to relieve congestion and encourage new growth.

RAMBLING Ramblers are vigorous roses which will climb, so are best trained up a structure or mature tree. During the

OPPOSITE AND PAGE 216 Pruning and tying in roses to wires and metal supports will encourage flowering, while creating interesting curved patterns or shapes with the stems can be done before plants begin to grow and flower **PAGE 217** *Rosa* 'Ghislaine de Féligonde' in summer

Late winter

215

growing season they will produce long, whippy stems which should be tied in to their support as these will flower the following year. Their vigorous growth can look untidy and be prone to damage, so prune in autumn, after they have finished flowering. Spent flowers should be cut off and old lateral stems can be shortened. On mature plants, remove one or two of the oldest main stems to encourage new growth.

CLIMBING These have a lax habit and so will require a support. They tend to be less vigorous than ramblers and their growth is often not as flexible. Many will repeat flower through summer and so can be deadheaded to encourage more blooms, although the main time to prune is in winter. Current season's growth can be shortened by half and laterals can be cut back to three or four buds. On established plants you may need to remove a couple of the oldest stems to alleviate congestion.

GROUNDCOVER These roses will naturally produce domes of foliage and flowers, and as a result require little pruning. In winter, plants can be reduced by shortening the most vigorous stems by a quarter. Lightly trim the rest to create symmetry.

A NOTE ON ROOTSTOCK SUCKERS Many roses are grafted; if this is the case, be mindful of rootstock suckers which may grow from the base of the plant or below the soil. These will look and flower differently to the main plant and once identified should be cut off at the base.

Prune fruit trees

Fruit trees don't immediately provide a generous yield, but given a little patience and care they will prove their worth tenfold. While producing an edible crop they also add much ornamental charm to a garden, whether it's their gnarled branches in winter or their attractive blossom in spring. An essential yearly task is pruning, which will help them remain healthy and productive. As with any pruning, the main principles should be considered first – remove dead, diseased and dying wood, followed by anything that is rubbing against another branch (see page 13).

Becoming familiar with how your tree grows will take time. Some varieties will naturally produce spurs (short fruiting branches) while others will produce long branches with fruit buds at the tips. Successful pruning will balance vegetative growth with fruiting. If you prune too hard you may remove too many of the fruiting buds and the tree will put all its energy into leafy growth the following year.

Apple and pear trees are perhaps the easiest to prune and should be cut back in winter. Once established, pear trees will require less pruning than apple trees as their growth tends to be more compact and upright. When pruning, look to improve air and light within the tree's canopy by removing up to one third of the overall growth. Main stems should be shortened by a third, pruning to an outward facing bud. Lateral stems can be cut back a little harder. If you have a young apple or pear tree, see formative pruning on page 13.

Apricots, nectarines and peaches are not as tough as other fruit trees and their early blossom can be prone to frost damage, so these are best given a sheltered position or grown in areas with mild winters. Peaches and apricots can also suffer from a fungal disease which deforms the leaves and so should be protected from the rain during winter and spring – growing them as fan-trained or dwarf forms in containers will make this easier. Being stone fruits, they should be pruned in late spring or early summer (see page 90). Remove sections of the oldest growth to relieve congestion and encourage new growth.

Summer pruning is used for various trained forms of fruit tree that require their growth to be restricted, as well as stone fruit (see summer pruning on page 90).

Prune climbing plants

Most climbing plants tend to be quite vigorous and have the ability to grow skywards, positioning themselves to take advantage of the best light conditions. In the garden these plants can become top heavy and, if left unchecked, they can swamp other plants and become a knotted mess of old stems and new growth. Regular pruning can prevent this, ensuring you get the best from your climbers without compromising the health of other plants. Different climbers require different methods of pruning, though with a little consideration and practice, it will become second nature to you.

CLEMATIS Before you start, determine which of the three groups your clematis belongs to. Group one flower in early spring on the previous year's growth and include the alpina, montana and winter-flowering clematis types. Pruning should be completed after flowering in mid-spring and involves lightly trimming stems back to strong buds, though trimming a few stems a little harder will encourage new growth from lower down. Group two include many of the large-flowered clematis cultivars, which are less vigorous. They flower on short shoots in late spring and early summer on the previous year's growth. These should be thinned lightly after flowering and again in late winter to stimulate new growth from lower down. To do this, prune back to strong buds, but note that pruning hard in winter will result in few flowers, so exercise restraint. Group three flower on the current season's growth in late summer. These include late, large-flowering types, along with small-flowering species and hybrids. Prune hard in late winter, cutting all stems back to about 40cm and completely removing any dead stems.

WISTERIA Pruning wisteria is often considered highly technical, though in reality it is quite simple and will dramatically improve flowering. Ornamental grapevines such as *Vitis coignetiae* (crimson glory vine) and *V. vinifera* 'Purpurea' (teinturier grape) can also be pruned using this method. During midsummer, trim back to six or seven leaves any long, soft growth that you do not require to form the main structure. After leaf fall in winter, prune lateral stems back to five buds; stems that are growing from the laterals should be shortened back to three buds. Any long, whippy growth coming from the main framework should be removed completely, unless required to develop the framework, in which case it should be shortened by about one third and tied into the desired position on the structure.

HONEYSUCKLE AND JASMINE Climbing honeysuckle and jasmine can be either early- or late-flowering, and evergreen or deciduous. The best time to prune all varieties is after flowering, either in summer for early-flowering types or in late winter for late-flowering types. In all cases, cut back up to one third of the outer growth that has flowered. Over time, the framework of both honeysuckle and jasmine will become woody and congested. When this happens, cut back all growth hard to the main stems, which will stimulate lots of fresh new growth that can be used to form the new framework (see restrictive pruning on page 13).

SHRUBS Some shrubs have a very relaxed habit and are good for training against walls and fences, much like climbers. These include abutilon, ceanothus, garrya, itea and pyracantha. Their pruning requirements vary, but as a general rule apply the main principles and remove dead, diseased and dying material after flowering.

TOP Tying vines into a secure framework is an essential yearly task **BOTTOM** *Clematis* 'Betty Corning' in late summer

Task list

Jobs to do during late winter

1

Force your rhubarb by covering the crowns of the plants so that the first growth develops in the dark – this makes it sweeter and more tender. Traditionally, a terracotta forcer is used for this job, although anything that excludes light will work. Take the forcer off after harvesting the first crop of tender stems in early spring and allow the plant to grow as normal.

2

If possible, coppice hazel and birch stems for use in early spring. Select well-branched stems that can be positioned, bent or woven to create structures that can support plants during the growing season (see page 36). If you don't have access to hazel or birch, this is the ideal time to buy lengths of both, as well as pea sticks and willow, from local suppliers.

3

Check on dahlia tubers (pictured) that have been lifted from the ground and stored in boxes in a garage or shed. Ensure they are not rotting or being eaten. Tubers can be potted up now in containers filled with dry compost. Leave them somewhere cold and dry to discourage growth. Only water them when you want them to start growing in spring.

4

Complete any winter pruning of shrubs that flowered in late summer, autumn or winter on the current season's growth (examples include buddleja, caryopteris and perovskia). Remove spent flowers, as well as some (up to one third) of the oldest structural growth, cutting at the base to encourage new growth and to reduce the overall size of the plant.

5

Check any tender plants that are overwintering inside or in a sheltered place; these may include auriculas, pelargoniums, salvias, succulents and cacti. Look out for slug and snail damage and remove any dead leaves, as these could become a source of mould. Keep plants dry, watering a little every week or two until the warmer weather arrives.

6

While things are quiet in the garden, clear, tidy and organise sheds and storage areas, checking that you have the correct equipment to make a good start when the growing season begins. Also check water features, irrigation systems and taps, ensuring they have not been damaged by frosts during the winter weather.

7

Complete remedial pruning of trees, checking for crossing branches and dead, diseased or dying wood. Low branches can be removed to 'lift' the canopy, improving growing conditions beneath by allowing more space and light to filter through.

8

Check previous gardening notes and list any new plants that you may want to add to the garden. Research varieties, source a supplier and order the plants so that they arrive in good time and you can plant them in spring.

9

Cut back herbaceous perennials and tidy borders in preparation for spring. This job can be left until early spring to avoid disturbing overwintering wildlife, but if the borders contain early spring bulbs, it is better completed now.

10

Prevent ponds and water features from completely freezing over by placing a floating object in the water. A couple of inflatable balls or even a floating bath duck will work. During the day the objects can be removed, allowing for gas exchange between the water and the atmosphere, as well as access for birds and other wildlife to drink.

11

Both bramble and ivy flowers are great for wildlife, but you may wish to control the size and spread of these plants. Spend time removing any overly rampant brambles and ivy that have crept into the garden unnoticed during the summer months. Where possible, try to dig up the roots as well as the top growth to prevent the plants regrowing.

12

Order and take advantage of bare-root stock that is available during the winter period. This includes roses, trees, herbaceous perennials and hedging. Cheaper to purchase, bare-root plants also have an increased vigour that is not usually matched by container-grown stock. These plants must be planted during late winter or early spring, before they begin growing.

Celebrate the season

Although this season is undoubtedly cold, I find it's still invigorating to don winter garb and go outside to enjoy what's on offer. It's amazing how a bracing walk or a view of the setting sun can lift the spirits, especially if a visit to a cosy pub is involved. With fewer flowers and leaves to distract me, my attention turns to the intricate world of moss, lichen and bark which take on many forms, colours and textures and are fascinating to research.

Though it may feel like everything is sleeping, squirrels, deer, foxes and other mammals brave the temperatures to forage and feed. It is also a great time to watch birds as our native populations are boosted by the arrival of migratory visitors. Various ducks, geese and swans arrive, while early dusk can bring sightings of hunting owls. The still, clear nights are also perfect for star gazing – check an online calendar for seasonal astronomical happenings, get a woolly hat and a flask of something warm ready, then head out to a high vantage point.

Harvest and forage

Brussels sprouts and kale reach their zenith during this time of year. The cold nights and frosts encourage these plants to convert more of their stored starches into sugars, enhancing their flavour. Standing unscathed through winter (provided the pigeons don't discover them), they are perfect for harvesting, adding much value to soups, roasts and pasta dishes. Whether you plan to grow them from small plants or seed sown in spring, look to interesting cultivars like kale 'Nero di Toscana' or Brussels sprout 'Ruby Crunch'. A must for me is the kale and sprout hybrid, often sold as 'flower sprouts' or 'kalette'.

Another crop that I couldn't do without at this time of year is Jerusalem artichoke. Grown like a perennial sunflower (although the flowers are inconspicuous and disappointing), this plant will put on tall growth during the growing season, creating tasty tubers below ground. In late autumn it can be cut back and the tubers lifted from the ground and either used fresh or stored for later use throughout winter (see page 147). By replanting a few tubers, you will ensure that you have a crop the following year. I particularly love them roasted with other roots such as celeriac (see page 201) and potatoes (see page 72), where their aromatic, smoky taste brings something special to the mix.

Observe a murmuration or roost

Late winter often brings harsh weather conditions that test both gardeners and the natural world. Many species have evolved techniques to survive, be it to hunker down and hibernate or migrate to a more favourable location. The latter is common for many bird species, which every year grace our shores providing additional interest and wonder for anyone who goes in search of them.

During late winter migratory starlings visit Britain from Scandinavia and Germany to take advantage of our relatively mild maritime weather. They bolster UK numbers, assembling to create an enormous flock known as a murmuration. By day the birds scatter, individually foraging in gardens and the countryside, only to gather in their thousands at the end of the day. Congregating above their roost site, the birds fly as one, creating a hypnotic, almost fluid and ever-changing shape in the sky.

The best time to witness a murmuration is during periods of cold weather in late winter, either in the morning, when the birds first take to the wing, or in early evening when they fly back to roost. Some good locations to witness this spectacle in the UK include Aberystwyth Pier in Aberystwyth, Albert Bridge in Belfast, Dungeness in Kent, Exe Estuary in Devon, Fairburn Ings in West Yorkshire and Leighton Moss in Lancashire.

Much like the starlings, crows, jackdaws and rooks also roost in large numbers. Again, migrant birds from northern and eastern Europe join their English counterparts during winter, sometimes increasing their numbers into the tens of thousands. The best time to see them is at dusk. While they lack the aerial acrobatics of the starlings, the magnitude of the flock makes this an incredible, breathtaking event to witness. Often located in eastern counties, some of the best sites to see these roosts include Buckenham Carrs in Norfolk, Hatton Castle in Aberdeenshire, Northward Hill in Kent and Bishop's Stortford in Hertfordshire.

Sing to bring in the new season

Ever since humans began to cultivate plants, they have had a strong relationship with nature, and in particular the seasons. Throughout different cultures and religions, many festivals and celebrations have evolved to observe and champion a specific season or time of year, and making a comeback is one such celebration: the ancient practice of wassailing.

Traditionally there were two types of wassailing. The first involved groups of partygoers going from house to house to sing songs and spread good will as they drank a warm ale, wine or cider from the wassail bowl. Where peasants sung to wealthy lords, gifts of food and drink were given in exchange for the songs and good blessings.

The second type is orchard wassailing. This involved songs and incantations being performed alongside a raised glass to toast the health of fruit trees and give thanks for a good harvest. Raucous noise is made by banging pots and pans beside a tree, which is believed to ward off any evil demons and awaken the tree spirits.

Today this practice has become a popular social gathering, bringing together communities in sleepy villages as well as those in towns and cities. The event usually takes place on the twelfth night (January 5) or more traditionally 'old twelvey' (January 17), which is the original twelfth night before the introduction of the Gregorian calendar.

Many now celebrate wassailing and a local event can usually be found online. Whether visiting houses, an orchard or singing to a river (as is the case in London), wassailing is a great excuse to get outside and have a drink, a laugh and sing with friends and strangers to mark the beginning of a new growing year.

Late winter

Index

Italic indicates an illustration; bold indicates a main entry.

Acknowledgements

Looking back, I remember the excitement of opening that first email, asking if I would be interested in writing a book about gardening and nature. Both have long been close to my heart, along with the creative aspects of writing, learning and teaching, so naturally my answer was an enthusiastic yes! The conversations, planning and work schedules that followed were rapid and now, just nine months later, it seems a little surreal to be writing this, knowing what has been produced.

This entire creative journey, for which I am truly grateful, would not have been possible were it not for my editor, Zena Alkayat. While making the initial introduction, Zena also pulled together a passionate and talented team, alongside encouraging and supporting me in writing this book. Kim Lightbody has lent her remarkable skill in photographing the garden, capturing the beauty and atmosphere in everyday details, while Sarah Pyke has artfully compiled image and text through gentle design in a way that harmoniously sits so comfortably on the page. I speak for all of us when I say I hope you enjoy this book.

Special thanks must also be given to my employers, as well as Rosemary Alexander, who kindly lent the use of their gardens and have encouraged me every step of my career. And to my parents who allowed me the time and freedom to discover what it is that I love doing. I must also mention my partner, who at times during this process has done more than his fair share of dog walking, cooking and cleaning. In the introduction, I speak of a gardening community, full of kind and generous individuals, who are always happy to share information and, on occasion, plants! I thank all of the gardeners, nurserymen, landscapers and designers that I have been fortunate enough to work alongside during my gardening journey so far. Happy growing.